Everyday AI

Simplifying Life With Artificial Intelligence

Bo Phelan

Table of Contents

Introduction

Artificial intelligence, once a concept confined to the pages of science fiction, has become an undeniable force shaping our daily lives. From the moment we check our smartphones in the morning to the way we navigate our world, AI is no longer a distant dream—it's here, changing how we live, work, and connect.

It opens up a world full of possibilities, yet it might also fill some with trepidation. It's not just about your phone predicting the next word you want to type or your smart home suggesting a playlist for Saturday morning chores. No, AI reaches beyond these conveniences, offering changes that promise to redefine our lifestyles, productivity, and self-improvement journeys.

However, are we equipped to embrace these changes, or does it all feel like too much too fast?

Artificial intelligence is at the core of this transformation, and whether you're an adult curious about technology, a professional seeking productivity hacks, or focused on personal growth, understanding AI isn't merely an option—it's a necessity. As our society becomes more automated, those who can harness AI to their benefit will find themselves thriving in ways once thought impossible.

This book aims to illuminate the practical applications of AI, dispelling myths while revealing its potential to enhance our lives. We'll explore how AI seamlessly integrates into our routines, from streamlining mundane household tasks to powering incredible personal growth. For adults overwhelmed by technology's complexity, we'll uncover user-friendly tools and techniques to simplify your experience. For busy professionals, discover how AI can transform productivity, freeing hours in your day to focus on what truly matters. And for those on a path of self-improvement, you'll be learning how AI technologies can be your ally in personal development, supporting everything from learning new skills to developing better habits.

Our journey begins with examining how AI functions intricately within the confines of our homes. One day in the near future you may find yourself waking up as your virtual assistant offers a report on weather conditions, suggests the best route to avoid traffic, and reminds you of critical appointments—all before you've even had your first sip of coffee. These aren't abstract concepts; rather, they are readily available innovations designed to enrich our quality of life. We'll look at specific examples and provide guidelines on selecting the right tools tailored to meet your lifestyle needs.

Next, we'll move into the workplace, where AI stands poised to overhaul how we work. In an era of constant connectivity and demanding schedules, professionals increasingly turn to AI-driven solutions to optimize their time management and productivity. From automating repetitive tasks to providing analytical insights that inform decision-making, AI empowers us to accomplish more, often with less effort. This section of the book will present actionable advice and real-world success stories demonstrating AI's transformative impact on modern business practices.

Finally, we'll explore one of the most exciting aspects of AI: its capacity to enhance our personal growth. Whether your goal is acquiring new knowledge, improving mental well-being, or developing healthier habits, AI offers personalized strategies to facilitate meaningful progress. Through intelligent coaching apps, adaptive learning platforms, and more, we will investigate how leveraging these technologies can accelerate self-development efforts, leading to authentic and lasting change.

Throughout this exploration, consider how AI intersects with the challenges you face daily. Which tasks drain your energy, leaving little time for passion projects or cherished relationships? How could AI alleviate that burden, affording you precious moments to devote to activities that bring joy and fulfillment? By encouraging reflection, this book intends to ignite curiosity and inspire confidence in adopting AI as an empowering tool.

Whether you're intrigued by AI's potential but wary of its complexities, driven by the need to boost efficiency in your career, or eager to unlock new dimensions in your personal evolution, this book serves as a guide and companion on your AI journey. Together, let's demystify artificial intelligence, recognizing it not just as a technology of tomorrow but as a valuable ally today. Join me as we embark on a captivating exploration of AI's role in reshaping our lives, equipping you with the insights and tools necessary to harness its capabilities for personal empowerment and enrichment.

While the road ahead may seem daunting, rest assured that each chapter provides clarity and information that will equip you with the knowledge to navigate this change confidently. By demystifying AI's complexities and highlighting its potential benefits, we aim to make this journey as accessible and rewarding as possible. Embrace the possibilities that lie ahead—as we peel back the layers of AI, you'll discover many ways it can enrich your life and empower you to thrive in an ever-changing world.

Chapter 1:

Understanding AI and

Its Potentials

It's not just a sci-fi dream; AI is reshaping our lives in real and tangible ways. From how we shop online to how we manage our day-to-day activities, AI seamlessly blends into our routines, transforming mundane processes into intuitive and interactive experiences. So, in the future, your devices will anticipate your needs even before you utter a word. As exciting as it sounds, this exploration of AI's potential offers much more than convenience—it opens doors to creativity, efficiency, and growth that were once beyond reach.

In this chapter, you'll explore AI's transformative capabilities and their impact on everyday life. We consider how AI systems learn from data to perform without step-by-step instructions, making them incredibly adaptable and smart. You'll see how AI technologies have evolved, tracing their roots and uncovering significant milestones that led us here.

The chapter also ventures into how AI plays a critical role across diverse industries, from healthcare diagnostics to personalized shopping suggestions. With a keen eye on practical applications, this exploration promises insights that are both relatable and inspiring for anyone eager to understand and leverage AI's vast potential.

Definition of AI and Its Historical Development

AI is a fascinating field that has captivated human imagination for decades, often depicted in science fiction as both wondrous and unsettling. At its core, AI is about creating machines that can simulate human intelligence. This involves systems capable of learning, problem-solving, understanding language, recognizing patterns, and even making decisions with minimal human intervention. From email spam filters and voice-activated assistants to more complex applications like autonomous vehicles and personalized shopping recommendations, AI manifests in numerous ways that enhance our daily experiences.

Understanding AI requires delving into its key components. These include machine learning, where computers can learn from data without explicit programming, and neural networks, inspired by the structure and functioning of the human brain. These processes enable AI systems to recognize patterns and make decisions. Over time, these technologies have become sophisticated, allowing machines to perform tasks that previously required human cognition. This technical advancement is foundational in defining AI today (What is the History of Artificial Intelligence (AI)? n.d.).

One of AI's most intriguing facets is its ability to evolve based on its interactions and data inputs. This adaptability means AI systems continue to improve their functionalities over time, becoming more efficient and accurate in their applications. Companies leverage these capabilities to enhance productivity and streamline operations, leading to innovations that redefine traditional business models.

The relevance of AI in everyday life is undeniable, offering tools that transform how we approach tasks, solve problems, and make decisions. Whether it's automating repetitive tasks at work, providing insights through data analysis, or enabling creative pursuits like music and art, AI has become an invaluable resource that broadens horizons and offers new possibilities.

History of AI

To truly appreciate AI's impact, we must explore its historical development. AI began long before it became a household term. In the early 20th century, the notion of artificial beings was popularized by media and literature, culminating in Karel Čapek's play "Rossum's Universal Robots" in 1921, which coined the term "robot." By 1950, Alan Turing had introduced The Turing Test, a method for evaluating a machine's ability to exhibit intelligent behavior equivalent to, or indistinguishable from, that of a human (The Evolution and Future of Artificial Intelligence: A Student's Guide, n.d.).

The evolution of AI continued through the subsequent decades with significant breakthroughs that reshaped technology. In 1956, John McCarthy organized the Dartmouth Conference, which officially marked the birth of artificial intelligence as a formal academic discipline. This era also saw the development of early AI programs, such as Arthur Samuel's checkers-playing program, which could improve its performance through experience—an early example of machine learning.

In the later decades of the 20th century, AI research experienced both rapid growth and challenges. The 1960s and '70s were periods of optimism, leading to the creation of advanced algorithms and machines capable of basic speech recognition and visual processing. However, limitations in computing power and unrealistic expectations led to an "AI winter," where funding and interest waned temporarily. Despite this, foundational work laid during these years proved crucial for future advancements.

It's essential to recognize how AI has adapted over different eras to meet societal needs. Initially focused on theoretical exploration, AI gradually shifted toward practical applications. Today, AI technologies are integrated across various sectors, influencing everything from healthcare to agriculture. In healthcare, for instance, AI aids in diagnosing diseases and personalizing treatment plans, increasing efficiency and accuracy. Similarly, in agriculture, AI-driven robotics help optimize yields and manage resources sustainably.

AI has become commonplace in recent years, often blending seamlessly into different industries and aspects of life. Many people might not realize how prevalent AI is because it functions so seamlessly behind the scenes. For instance, when you ask your smartphone's virtual assistant for directions, AI processes your request and provides a well-informed response almost instantaneously. In e-commerce, AI analyzes your browsing habits to recommend products you'll likely be interested in, enhancing your shopping experience.

Current Trends in AI Technologies

AI has swiftly become a cornerstone of our modern world, influencing how we create, work, and interact. To effectively navigate this AI-powered future, individuals and organizations must understand these developments and adapt accordingly. Embracing generative AI and its integration into daily life requires a willingness to explore new possibilities and redefine conventional workflows. As AI tools become more accessible and user-friendly, people from various backgrounds can leverage them to boost personal productivity, professional output, and creative endeavors.

Generative AI

Among the emerging trends reshaping the landscape today is generative AI, which introduces transformative changes across various fields by creating new digital content. Generative AI models, leveraging powerful algorithms and vast datasets, enable machines to generate original works like text, music, images, and even code. This capability augments human creativity and catalyzes efficiency in tasks previously deemed too complex or time-consuming for automation.

These models have found widespread applications, from assisting writers with idea generation to enabling artists to experiment with new styles effortlessly. For instance, GPT-4 and similar tools have been instrumental in creating human-like dialogue, which facilitates innovative storytelling in books, films, and video games. Such advancements underpin the massive growth projected for the AI market, emphasizing the role of generative AI as a core technology that continues to revolutionize content creation across industries (Malec, 2024).

Integration Into Everyday Software and Devices

As AI becomes commonplace, it seeps into everyday applications, enhancing the functionality of common software and devices. This integration demonstrates AI's embedded role in our daily lives, often going unnoticed by the users who benefit from its capabilities. Smartphones offer a prime example; they employ AI for functions like photo recognition, virtual assistance, and predictive typing, which streamline user interaction and improve accessibility.

Incorporating AI into these systems illustrates its potential to make technology more intuitive and foolproof. Devices like smart speakers, home appliances, and navigation systems utilize voice recognition and natural language processing to perform tasks efficiently and accurately. Such features simplify multitasking and enable a seamless lifestyle experience, empowering users to save time and effort in mundane activities once considered labor-intensive (Coursera Staff, 2025).

Guidelines for utilizing AI in everyday applications stress the importance of balancing automation with human oversight. Users should remain informed about the data being generated and shared, maintaining control over privacy and ethical considerations. Meanwhile, businesses should prioritize upskilling their workforce to complement AI systems, fostering collaboration between humans and artificial intelligence to drive innovation sustainably.

AI in Business and Industry

Beyond personal devices, AI's presence is increasingly felt across various industries aiming for operational efficiency. From automating routine tasks to providing precision in decision-making processes, AI enhances productivity and accuracy in sectors like healthcare, finance, manufacturing, and retail. In healthcare, AI-driven diagnostics and data analysis allow for earlier disease detection and personalized treatment plans, improving patient outcomes while reducing costs.

In the financial industry, AI algorithms assist in risk assessment, fraud detection, and personalized customer services, contributing to safer and more tailored financial solutions. Manufacturing benefits from AI through predictive maintenance and supply chain optimization, minimizing downtime, and streamlining production processes. Retailers leverage AI to analyze consumer behavior, optimize inventory management, and personalize marketing strategies, boosting customer satisfaction and sales performance. These examples underscore the broad applicability of AI technologies in advancing business objectives and setting significant trends in numerous sectors (Malec, 2024).

Data

Supporting the breakthroughs in AI is the crucial role of data, serving as the lifeblood that powers these advanced technologies. The availability and quality of data directly influence AI's effectiveness and its range of applications. With the explosion of big data, AI systems can be trained on diverse datasets to enhance their learning and adaptability, leading to more sophisticated and contextually aware models.

Data's importance cannot be overstated, as it not only fuels innovation but also determines the reliability and decision-making capabilities of AI solutions. For AI to be beneficial across different domains, it must rely on accurate, representative data that reflects real-world conditions and variances. Companies investing in robust data infrastructures are better positioned to harness AI's full potential, aligning it with strategic goals and ensuring competitive advantages in an ever-evolving market landscape (Coursera Staff, 2025).

Understanding Machine Learning and Neural Networks

When we talk about AI, it's easy to think of it as a complex technology that seems out of reach. But at its core, AI is about systems learning from data to carry out tasks without being explicitly programmed for each step. One of the most vital techniques enabling AI today is machine learning and the interrelated fields of neural networks and deep learning.

Machine Learning

Machine learning is the backbone of AI's capability to learn and adapt independently. For instance, say you were to teach a child to identify animals. Instead of giving a detailed description of each animal, you show them pictures over time, allowing them to recognize patterns and classify new images effortlessly. Machine learning works similarly; it processes large sets of data, learns patterns, and improves performance on tasks like image recognition or language translation without needing human intervention at every stage.

To see machine learning in action, consider everyday scenarios. Take personalized recommendations on platforms like Netflix or Amazon. Thanks to machine learning algorithms, these services analyze your habits and suggest content tailored to your tastes, often introducing you to something you didn't know you'd enjoy. This approach isn't just limited to entertainment; digital assistants like Siri or Alexa rely on machine learning to interpret voice commands, set reminders, or control smart home devices seamlessly. These examples illustrate machine learning's adaptation to improve user experience effortlessly.

Neural Networks

Central to machine learning are neural networks, inspired by the intricate web of neurons in our brain. Your brain processes thousands of inputs as you navigate daily life—recognizing faces, interpreting meanings, and even making quick decisions. Neural networks emulate this process mathematically, using layers of interconnected nodes to weigh input data and produce outputs. They enable machines to grasp complex features such as voice commands or facial recognition, making it seem like they "understand."

A good analogy for neural networks would be how humans teach their brains to process complex information efficiently, like learning a new language. Initially, it might be challenging, but with practice, the brain begins to recognize patterns—conjugation rules, syntax structures—eventually holding a conversation fluently. Neural networks improve similarly, refining their decision-making with more data exposure. Their ability to tackle tasks with human-like logic makes them invaluable in today's tech-driven world.

Deep Learning

Yet machine learning doesn't stop with recommendations. We enter deeper layers with deep learning, a subset of machine learning focused on achieving even higher capabilities. While traditional machine learning might stop after recognizing basic features, deep learning incorporates various layers to enhance understanding intricately. Imagine peeling an onion, where each layer adds more depth. Similarly, deep learning involves multiple processing layers, enabling machines to understand abstract concepts, make predictions, and perform tasks once thought exclusive to humans.

Consider how deep learning drives advancements in autonomous vehicles. Through numerous training experiences, these systems distinguish complex driving conditions—like navigating busy intersections or recognizing pedestrians in various lighting. The depth of understanding enables them to make split-second safety decisions, heralding a new era of transportation.

Another compelling application is medical diagnostics. Deep learning models analyze medical images or patient histories, assisting doctors in early disease detection. Their precision in recognizing subtle signs enhances diagnostic accuracy, saving lives through timely interventions.

AI Ethics and Societal Impacts

Understanding the ethical considerations and societal implications of AI technology is essential for anyone engaging with these transformative systems. In recent years, AI's rapid expansion has sparked discussions about its ethical use, bringing to light concerns regarding fairness, transparency, and accountability in AI technologies. Ethical AI principles serve as a guide to help developers create systems that are not only effective but also conscientious and responsible.

Biases in Data

One key aspect of ethical AI involves addressing biases that can be present in data used for training machine learning models. These biases often reflect social inequalities, which could lead to discriminatory outcomes in automated decisions. For example, facial recognition technologies have been observed to produce less accurate results for individuals with darker skin tones, posing risks of unequal treatment (The Ethical Considerations of Artificial Intelligence, 2023). Therefore, AI practitioners must conduct bias detection and mitigation processes regularly to ensure fair treatment across diverse groups.

Fostering inclusivity in AI development processes can result in more comprehensive and empathetic technologies. Diverse teams bring varied perspectives, contributing to solutions that better address the needs of different user demographics. Encouraging underrepresented groups to enter and thrive within the tech industry is crucial for achieving this diversity of thought and experience.

Job Automation

In addition to ethical standards, adopting AI also impacts societal dynamics, particularly employment. The concern over job displacement due to automation is legitimate, as AI systems increasingly replace repetitive and manual tasks. This shift necessitates proactive strategies to manage transitional phases, such as government and industry initiatives to retrain workers and prepare them for new, AI-related roles. While some positions may be lost, others will emerge, requiring skills that intersect with technology, creativity, and human-centric problem-solving (Verma, 2023).

AI, Digital Communication, and Deepfakes

AI's influence has reshaped how we interact socially and culturally. Consider how digital assistants like Siri or Alexa have changed our communication habits. Similarly, AI's capacity to generate realistic media through technologies like deepfakes raises questions about authenticity and trust in information dissemination. Such shifts call for a recalibration of societal norms and expectations around interaction and content consumption.

To navigate these challenges effectively, risk mitigation strategies must be part of AI adoption plans. Whether at an organizational or personal level, establishing frameworks that prioritize security, privacy, and transparency is vital. Companies should implement robust data protection measures to safeguard sensitive information against breaches and misuse. Additionally, creating systems with clear accountability mechanisms enables users to understand and react appropriately when AI-driven outcomes do not align with intended purposes.

Guidelines and Regulations

Regulations and guidelines play a significant role in providing direction for ethical AI use. International collaborations among technologists, policymakers, and ethicists are essential for developing global standards and policies. For instance, deploying autonomous weapons without strict accountability could lead to catastrophic consequences, necessitating stringent international agreements (The Ethical Considerations of Artificial Intelligence, 2023). By imposing clear regulations, stakeholders can work together to prevent the potential misuse of AI technologies.

When harnessed responsibly, AI holds immense potential for innovation across various sectors, from healthcare to education, agriculture to finance. It can assist in diagnosing diseases earlier, customizing learning experiences for students, boosting agricultural productivity, and optimizing financial forecasts. Envisioning this future involves raising awareness and educating communities on the possibilities and limitations of AI, ensuring that everyone has the opportunity to participate and benefit.

Final Insights

Throughout this chapter, we've looked at the foundational aspects of artificial intelligence, unraveling its historical development and how it has evolved to become a transformative force in our daily lives. From early representations of AI in fiction to groundbreaking milestones like The Turing Test and machine learning innovations, we traced the journey that brought AI to where it stands today. Nowadays AI is not just a concept for tech enthusiasts but a practical tool that seamlessly integrates into various aspects of our routines—from simplifying everyday tasks with virtual assistants to enhancing personalized experiences across different sectors.

Embracing AI's potential means understanding its adaptability and creativity in reshaping how we approach activities. By leveraging AI technologies, whether it's optimizing work processes or personal growth pursuits, we can unlock new efficiencies and avenues for innovation. With its continued advancement, AI promises to remain an integral part of our future, offering possibilities that extend beyond automation to enrich our professional and personal lives. As we move forward, staying informed and open-minded about AI's applications is crucial in harnessing its benefits while navigating its challenges responsibly.

Chapter 2:

Streamlining Household Tasks

Streamlining household tasks can be overwhelming, where demands on our time are constantly increasing. As we juggle work commitments, family responsibilities, and personal interests, any opportunity to simplify our daily routines can be immensely beneficial.

 Would you like a home that automatically adapts to your needs, freeing up precious minutes each day for activities you truly enjoy?

With the advent of AI, transforming such imaginings into reality is no longer just a dream— it's reality. AI's potential to seamlessly integrate into domestic life offers a way to reclaim time spent on mundane chores, allowing us to focus on the things that matter most.

In this chapter, we'll explore how AI enhances household management by simplifying tasks that once required constant attention. From smart devices making energy-saving decisions to AI-driven cleaning tools tackling dirt without human intervention, the possibilities are endless. You'll discover practical applications of AI designed to suit various aspects of everyday living, helping you achieve greater efficiency and convenience with minimal effort. We'll also explore the role of voice-activated assistants, which revolutionize tasks by providing hands-free control over numerous household functions.

Whether you're interested in improving productivity, achieving a better work-life balance, or simply embracing modern technology for self-improvement, this chapter aims to provide valuable insights and actionable advice to enhance your home experience through AI innovation.

Smart Home Devices and Automation

Smart home devices present a remarkable opportunity to enhance daily living through automation and efficiency. By embracing smart home technology, you can gain valuable time back in your day. Automating routine tasks minimizes the mental load of managing a household, freeing up time for other essential activities or relaxation. Additionally, smart devices encourage proactive approaches to energy management and sustainability, fostering responsible consumption habits that align with self-improvement initiatives.

We'll look at a few of the most innovative smart home devices to come onto the market in recent years below.

The Smart Thermostat

One of the most revolutionary products in the home sector is the smart thermostat. These devices go beyond simple temperature control by offering automated management that increases both energy savings and personal comfort. If you own a smart thermostat you come home to a perfectly warm or cool house at precisely the right moment without lifting a finger.

With features like geofencing, smart thermostats detect when the home is empty and adjust accordingly, which significantly reduces energy consumption. The ability to monitor and control your home's temperature remotely means you can optimize settings even when you're away, ensuring both comfort and cost-effectiveness (Jantz-Sell, 2024).

For those who are budget-conscious, beginning with an Energy Star-certified smart thermostat can be a strategic starting point for reducing energy use. This is because heating and cooling typically make up the largest share of household energy consumption (Jantz-Sell, 2024). Such thoughtful innovation helps lower energy bills while maintaining personalized settings that prioritize individual comfort.

Smart Lighting Systems

Smart lighting systems further simplify our lives by automating light throughout the home. Gone are the days of manually flipping switches or leaving lights on unnecessarily. Smart lighting offers convenience by allowing control from your mobile devices. This level of control enhances home security by giving the impression that someone is at home and significantly reduces electricity usage. The integration of voice assistants allows users to manage lighting with simple commands, adding another layer of ease to home management. Investing in Energy Star-certified smart lights presents an inexpensive way to start your smart home journey and can seamlessly integrate with existing systems and routines (Jantz-Sell, 2024).

Smart Security Systems

Security is definitely of utmost importance in any home. Smart security systems elevate safety measures to new heights. With AI-driven real-time alerts and monitoring, homeowners are no longer tethered to traditional alarm systems. Smart locks, cameras, and sensors provide instant notifications of any unusual activity, enabling immediate action. These systems often include features that allow remote locking or unlocking of doors and even recording of access attempts. Not only does this improve home security, but it also offers peace of mind for individuals constantly on the go (What is a Smart Home and What are the Benefits?, 2025).

Home Automation Hubs

Central to the operation of various smart devices is the home automation hub. A hub acts as the command center, unifying different components into a cohesive system. Through these hubs, users can enjoy seamless integration of all connected devices, streamlining their management into a single interface. By centralizing control, it's possible to create customized schedules or automate routines based on occupancy and preferences. This not only simplifies day-to-day operations but also contributes to enhanced energy efficiency by ensuring devices operate optimally and reduce unnecessary power use (Jantz-Sell, 2024).

Guidance

The choice to transition to a smart home environment need not be overwhelming. By identifying specific needs and gradually introducing compatible smart products, homeowners can transform their spaces at their own pace. Starting small with devices such as smart plugs or lights allows you to experience the benefits firsthand before expanding to more comprehensive solutions. As you become familiar with how these technologies interact and function, you can continue to incrementally build a smart network tailored to your lifestyle and efficiency goals (What is a Smart Home and What are the Benefits?, 2025).

AI-Driven Cleaning Tools

AI-driven cleaning tools are advanced devices that utilize artificial intelligence to enhance cleaning efficiency and effectiveness. They can include robotic vacuum cleaners, smart mops, and other automated cleaning solutions. Finding ways to streamline household tasks is crucial for many individuals. AI has rapidly emerged as a valuable tool for automating various cleaning chores, saving time and energy.

Key features of AI-driven cleaning tools include:

1. **Navigation and Mapping:** Using sensors and cameras, these devices can map out spaces, identify obstacles, and create optimized cleaning paths for thorough coverage.

2. **Adaptive Cleaning:** AI algorithms allow these tools to learn from their environment, adjusting their cleaning strategies based on the type of surfaces or the amount of dirt detected.

3. **Scheduling and Control:** Many AI-driven cleaning devices can be controlled remotely via smartphone apps, allowing users to schedule cleanings, monitor progress, and customize settings.

4. **Voice Activation:** Integration with smart home systems enables users to command the cleaners using voice assistants like Amazon Alexa or Google Assistant.

5. **Data Collection:** Some devices can collect data on cleaning habits, providing insights into how often different areas need cleaning or identifying high-traffic zones.

Overall, AI-driven cleaning tools aim to make cleaning more efficient and reduce the manual effort required, providing convenience for busy households.

Now, let's explore the AI devices that can transform the way we manage cleaning tasks in our homes.

The Robotic Vacuum Cleaner

One of the most popular AI innovations in home cleaning is the robotic vacuum cleaner. These devices automatically clean floors, effectively navigating around furniture and obstacles. By employing sensors and AI algorithms, robotic vacuums map out your floor plan and determine the most efficient cleaning path. This capability saves time, and for those who dread manual vacuuming, this technology provides an effortless alternative, allowing you to focus on more important activities (Kumar, 2025).

Smart Mops

Smart mops take automated floor cleaning a step further by combining vacuuming and mopping functions. Devices like the Ecovacs Deebot X8 Pro Omni offer advanced features such as dual water tanks and automated control of water usage, optimizing the cleaning process. These smart mops adjust to different floor types and are equipped with intelligent mapping systems that adapt to various room layouts. This versatility makes them suitable for homes with diverse flooring needs, ensuring a thorough and customized cleaning experience. Moreover, their ability to switch automatically between vacuuming and mopping enhances efficiency, further reducing the need for manual intervention (Kumar, 2025).

Dishwashers With AI Integration

Dishwashers have also evolved with AI integration, leading to the development of AI-powered dishwashers that optimize washing cycles. Traditional dishwashers often use excessive amounts of water and energy, which can be wasteful. In contrast, AI models analyze variables such as load size, soil level, and type of dishes to adjust settings accordingly. This optimization results in greater efficiency and resource savings, without compromising cleaning performance. For environmentally conscious homeowners, AI-powered dishwashers present a more sustainable option while still providing immaculate results.

Window Cleaning Robots

One often overlooked cleaning task is window cleaning, which can be labor-intensive and challenging when dealing with high or hard-to-reach windows. However, window-cleaning robots provide a safe and efficient solution. Equipped with intelligent sensors and suction technologies, these robots attach securely to windows and navigate across surfaces to remove dirt and grime. They eliminate the hazards associated with climbing ladders and allow streak-free cleaning by detecting edges and adjusting their paths accordingly. With options like the Tosima W2, users can choose from various cleaning modes and enjoy sparkling windows without any physical effort.

Energy Management With AI

In our modern homes, AI is quietly revolutionizing how we manage energy consumption, bringing both cost savings and sustainability right to our doorsteps. By integrating smart technologies, homeowners can not only keep track of their energy use but also make smart adjustments that lead to more efficient and eco-friendly lifestyles.

Smart Energy Monitors

One of the forefront innovations in this area is the deployment of smart energy monitors. These devices provide real-time data on household energy usage, allowing residents to see exactly how much power each appliance consumes at any given moment. This visibility transforms abstract ideas about electricity usage into concrete metrics, empowering homeowners with the knowledge they need to make informed decisions about their energy consumption habits. By understanding which appliances draw the most current and when, individuals can develop strategies to reduce their overall energy use, leading to lower utility bills and a smaller carbon footprint (Home Energy Management System (HEMS), 2024).

Automated Energy Management Systems

Building on the foundation laid by smart energy monitors, automated energy management systems take conservation a step further by dynamically adapting how energy is used throughout the day. These systems analyze patterns of consumption and adjust based on factors such as peak periods when electricity rates are highest. For instance, these systems mean you can program your washing machine to automatically start its cycle during off-peak hours or your AC unit to pre-cool your home just before temperatures rise in the afternoon— these are examples of how automation can fine-tune daily energy use without compromising comfort.

Solar Energy Management

Another significant advancement is solar energy management, which uses AI to optimize the use of solar power according to weather forecasts and predicted energy needs. By harnessing the sun's power efficiently, homes equipped with solar panels can maximize their use of renewable energy and minimize reliance on the grid. The AI component learns from past weather data and current forecasts to predict solar production and suggests the best times to run energy-intensive appliances. Not only does this practice promote the use of sustainable energy, but it also reduces electricity costs over time since more solar power is consumed rather than sold back to the grid (Schneider Electric Launches AI-Powered Home Energy Management Feature for Wiser Home, 2024).

Smart Outlets and Plugs

Smart outlets and plugs play an important role in optimizing home energy use. These devices allow homeowners to control and schedule when electrical outlets supply power to connected appliances remotely. By setting schedules through user-friendly apps, individuals can prevent energy waste from appliances left running unnecessarily. For instance, they can ensure that lamps, coffee makers, and other electronics are turned off when not needed or activate them shortly before arrival home. This control not only saves energy but also provides added convenience for busy households.

Potential Savings

The potential savings from these technologies are significant. Automated systems and smart devices enable what can be described as a proactive approach to energy management. They encourage users to think differently about energy consumption—not as a fixed demand but as a variable that can be optimized. As a result, households can experience substantial reductions in monthly energy bills and contribute positively to environmental conservation efforts by reducing emissions associated with traditional power generation (Home Energy Management System (HEMS), 2024).

Voice-Activated Assistants for Everyday Tasks

Voice-activated assistants have revolutionized the way we manage household tasks by simplifying daily activities and enhancing productivity. These smart devices serve as personal assistants equipped with various capabilities that enhance different areas of our lives, from setting reminders to accessing entertainment.

Some examples of voice-activated AI assistants include:

- **Amazon Alexa:** Found in Amazon Echo devices, Alexa can control smart home devices, provide information, play music, and more through voice commands.

- **Google Assistant:** Integrated into Google Home devices and many smartphones, Google Assistant helps with tasks like setting reminders, answering questions, and controlling smart devices.

- **Apple Siri:** Available on Apple devices, Siri can send messages, play music, provide directions, and control other smart devices using voice commands.

- **Microsoft Cortana:** Although mainly focused on productivity, Cortana can perform tasks, manage calendars, and control smart devices using voice input.

- **Samsung Bixby:** Found on Samsung devices, Bixby can assist with phone functions, smart home controls, and providing information through voice commands.

- **Baidu DuerOS:** Popular in China, DuerOS is a voice-activated assistant that helps with various tasks, ranging from smart home control to providing information and entertainment.

These AI assistants are designed to make daily tasks easier and enhance user convenience through voice interaction. Let's delve into how these assistants transform our routines and make life more manageable.

Time Management

One of the key benefits of voice-activated assistants is their ability to assist in time management through setting reminders and alarms. With just a simple voice command, you can schedule appointments, set medication reminders, or even create wake-up calls. This functionality ensures you stay on top of your daily tasks without the need to manually jot down notes or constantly check a calendar. By vocalizing tasks, individuals can focus more on their activities while staying organized, enhancing both efficiency and punctuality (Tsymbal, 2024).

Voice-Activated Shopping Lists

Incorporating voice-based shopping lists is another ingenious way these assistants streamline everyday errands. Gone are the days of scribbling down grocery lists on paper. Now, you can effortlessly add items to your shopping list by speaking directly to your device. Some assistants can even connect with grocery delivery services, allowing you to order essentials without lifting a finger. This seamless integration reduces time spent on planning trips and organizing purchases, making grocery shopping a breeze(Senyk, 2024)!

Hands-Free Connectivity

The convenience extends beyond individual tasks through hands-free home connectivity, which allows for greater control over household functions. With voice commands, you can adjust lighting, modify thermostat settings, or even lock doors—all without interrupting what you're currently doing. This feature provides improved accessibility, especially for family members who might find traditional methods challenging. For instance, parents can control the environment while tending to children, and elderly or disabled family members gain independence in operating household devices.

Multitasking

Moreover, voice-activated technology enhances multitasking by enabling easy access to information and entertainment. Whether you're cooking dinner or working on a project, you can request news updates, play music, or even ask for a recipe without needing to stop what you're doing. This capability proves invaluable in maintaining productivity as it allows users to absorb content and perform tasks simultaneously, effectively using each moment to the fullest. Busy professionals and tech enthusiasts alike benefit from this constant flow of information and media without having to divert attention from primary tasks. (Tsymbal, 2024)

Practical application of these functions illustrates how voice assistants can be seamlessly integrated into our routines. For example, if you are cooking dinner with your hands full simply ask your assistant for measurement conversions or step-by-step instructions. As you wrap up your evening, you can effortlessly schedule reminders for upcoming meetings or chores. Before bedtime, a quick voice command can set the alarm for the next day, turn off lights, and lower the thermostat for a comfortable sleep. These small yet significant actions accumulate, promoting an organized and smoother lifestyle.

Final Insights

As we've explored in this chapter, integrating AI into household management can transform mundane tasks into effortlessly efficient routines. By adopting smart home technologies like energy-saving thermostats and automated lighting systems, you're cutting down on energy costs and simplifying daily chores. These devices work quietly behind the scenes to optimize your environment, providing comfort and convenience without constant manual oversight. For those who are feeling cautious about diving into tech, starting small with individual smart products can be a simple and rewarding first step.

Moreover, AI-driven cleaning tools and voice-activated assistants further enrich our day-to-day lives by tackling tedious tasks and offering seamless control over home functions. Whether it's a robotic vacuum keeping your floors spotless or a voice assistant managing your schedule, the benefits of these innovations are clear. They free up valuable time and mental space, allowing you to focus on what truly matters. As you continue to integrate smart solutions into your home, you'll find that these advancements not only make life more manageable but also encourage sustainable living habits and personal growth. Embracing these changes can lead to a smarter, more connected home and a happier, more balanced lifestyle.

Chapter 3:

Boosting Workplace Productivity

Boosting workplace productivity is now more feasible than ever with the rise of innovative AI tools designed to enhance professional efficiency and collaboration. As businesses constantly evolve, leveraging technology to stay competitive isn't just an option; it's a necessity.

Adopting AI technology in the workplace means that tasks like scheduling meetings, updating status reports, or even predicting project challenges are no longer on your plate. AI is shifting the focus from routine chores to strategic, high-impact activities. Professionals have access to powerful tools that streamline workflow and provide new ways to connect and collaborate with team members, regardless of their location.

Here, we'll look into ways artificial intelligence is revolutionizing how we manage projects and resources at work. We'll explore various AI applications, starting with the automation of mundane tasks that free up valuable time for employees to concentrate on innovation and growth. You'll learn about AI's role in optimizing resource allocation, ensuring that every aspect of a project is executed with precision and minimal waste.

Discover how real-time tracking and predictive analytics offer insights into potential risks, empowering teams to tackle challenges head-on. By examining these exciting developments, you'll gain a better understanding of how AI can be harnessed to boost productivity and foster a more dynamic and efficient work environment.

AI for Project Management

In today's rapidly evolving work environments, artificial intelligence is significantly transforming project management processes by streamlining tasks and enhancing team collaboration. AI's capabilities in automating routine activities empower teams to spend less time on mundane chores and more on strategic endeavors that drive innovation and success.

Task Automation

Task automation refers to employing AI tools to handle repetitive and time-consuming tasks such as data entry, scheduling, or status updates. By automating these activities, teams can redirect their focus towards more creative and strategic aspects of their projects.

For example, many companies are now using AI-driven project management tools to automatically schedule meetings, update task statuses, or even send reminders to team members. This not only saves time but also ensures consistency and accuracy across project timelines. Automating these low-value tasks reduces the cognitive load on employees, allowing them to utilize their skills for higher-value tasks, ultimately boosting productivity and job satisfaction.

Resource Allocation

Beyond routine tasks, AI plays an integral role in resource allocation. Effective resource allocation is crucial for managing any project as it involves distributing time, budget, and human resources optimally to ensure successful project outcomes. AI-driven tools can analyze historical project data and current workload to predict future resource needs. They can suggest optimal distribution strategies based on existing constraints, helping managers make informed decisions about resource utilization. These recommendations are often more accurate than those made by humans due to AI's ability to process large volumes of disparate data swiftly.

Tools like Celoxis AI offer scenario-based planning features, allowing managers to simulate different resource allocation scenarios and choose the most effective one (Das, 2024). This precision prevents resource overuse and improves cost efficiency, contributing to better project completion rates and minimized waste.

Real-Time Tracking of Project Progress

AI's contribution extends to real-time tracking of project progress which is a critical aspect of modern project management. Real-time tracking allows project managers to maintain continual oversight over their projects, offering instant visibility into progress and pinpointing potential bottlenecks before they escalate into significant issues. Advanced AI monitoring systems provide dashboards that display live project metrics, like task progress, resource utilization, and adherence to budgetary limits. Managers can gain comprehensive insights simply by asking systems like Celoxis AI questions such as, "What's causing the delay in Task 4?" (AI in Project Management: Streamlining Tasks and Automation, 2024). Further, these tools can dynamically adjust schedules based on actual progress, reallocating resources as needed to keep projects on track, reducing delays, and maintaining momentum.

Predictive Analytics

Predictive analytics powered by AI revolutionizes how potential project challenges are addressed, turning what used to be an uncertain predictive exercise into a structured forecast based on robust data analysis. Predictive analytics leverages past data to identify trends, uncover potential risks, and estimate timelines or budgets with greater precision. This foresight enables project managers to proactively address possible hurdles, whether it's timeline delays, budget overruns, or resource shortages. By anticipating these challenges, teams can develop contingency plans, allocate buffer resources, or adjust timelines well in advance, reducing the risk of project derailments.

Consider the example of a project manager using AI tools to prepare a project timeline. With access to data from previous similar projects, the AI tool can provide suggestions on potential risks and recommend adjustments based on historical performance indicators. If a resource constraint is anticipated, AI can immediately propose alternatives, like reallocating staff or adjusting workloads, minimizing the need for reactive problem-solving when issues arise. Such enhanced predictive capabilities lead to more confidence in decision-making processes, empowering teams to take calculated risks and embrace innovative strategies without fear of unexpected setbacks.

Virtual Assistants in the Workplace

Enhancing productivity is a top priority for professionals and businesses alike. Virtual assistants improve workplace efficiency by taking over mundane yet essential tasks, freeing up time for employees to focus on more strategic and creative endeavors. This section highlights how virtual assistants optimize scheduling, information retrieval, communication management, and task delegation, ultimately contributing to a more streamlined and productive workflow.

Optimize Scheduling

One of the most significant advantages of employing a virtual assistant is their ability to handle scheduling and reminders effectively. Managing appointments, meetings, and deadlines can become overwhelming, especially as business operations grow in complexity. Virtual assistants minimize the risk of scheduling conflicts by efficiently organizing calendars and setting up timely reminders. This ensures that employees and executives are always aware of upcoming tasks and commitments, leading to better time management and reduced stress. As they juggle everyday tasks to grow and scale their operations, virtual assistants serve as valuable support systems, leveraging project management tools to keep everything organized and on track (Clarkson, 2024).

Improved Information Retrieval

In information retrieval, virtual assistants offer quick and easy access to necessary data and files. In traditional settings, employees may spend substantial amounts of time searching through emails or databases to find the relevant information needed for decision-making processes. Virtual assistants, equipped with efficient search capabilities and organization skills, can swiftly locate and retrieve information, allowing employees to make informed decisions promptly.

This rapid access to information enhances productivity, as it eliminates downtime associated with manual searches, ensuring that team members can continue working seamlessly without unnecessary interruptions. By automating repetitive tasks such as data entry and document retrieval, virtual assistants facilitate more efficient use of human resources and contribute to improved operational efficiency (Top 10 Benefits of a Virtual Assistant, n.d.).

Streamlined Communication Management

Communication management is another area where virtual assistants prove invaluable. Teams often face challenges in maintaining clear and consistent communication, which can lead to misunderstandings and information loss. Virtual assistants help streamline communication flows by managing emails, setting up meetings, and facilitating team discussions. They ensure that important messages are not overlooked and that all parties remain updated on critical developments.

This optimization of communication pathways nurtures a more collaborative work environment, reducing inefficiencies and enhancing overall team dynamics. Virtual assistants also integrate with various communication platforms, ensuring seamless interactions across different teams or departments, further boosting productivity and collaboration (Clarkson, 2024).

Smooth Task Delegation

Virtual assistants also play a crucial role in task delegation. Delegating tasks accurately is vital for maintaining workflow efficiency and ensuring that projects are completed on time. Virtual assistants aid in assigning tasks clearly and effectively, making sure that each team member knows their responsibilities and deadlines. This clarity not only promotes a sense of accountability among employees but also helps avoid overlap or duplication of efforts. Through organized task management, virtual assistants contribute to smoother project execution and enhanced team performance. When using project management tools like Asana or Trello, virtual assistants provide an additional layer of organization, tracking progress and keeping everyone aligned with their goals (Clarkson, 2024).

Automation of Repetitive and Administrative Tasks

Virtual assistants' ability to automate repetitive or administrative tasks frees up employees to focus on higher-level strategic initiatives and value-added activities. Professionals can dedicate their attention to core business functions, innovative problem-solving, and strategic planning, leading to better outcomes and the potential for business growth. The delegation of routine responsibilities allows teams to operate more efficiently, ensuring that energy and resources are directed toward activities that drive success and innovation (Clarkson, 2024).

Automated Data Analysis and Reporting

AI has emerged as a cornerstone in the transformation of data analysis and reporting processes, significantly improving workplace productivity. By automating these tasks, AI not only speeds up operations but also enhances the quality of decision-making within an organization. Below, we look at how AI-driven solutions collect, analyze, and report data to produce actionable insights that aid strategic planning and continuous improvement.

Automated Data Collection

The first step towards leveraging AI for improved decision-making is automated data collection. Traditionally, gathering data from multiple sources could be a labor-intensive process fraught with human error. However, AI systems are designed to seamlessly integrate with various data points, extracting information swiftly and accurately. This automation eliminates the manual effort involved in data gathering, saving crucial time and preserving resources. By ensuring high data quality, AI allows analysts to base their conclusions on robust datasets, leading to more accurate and reliable insights (AI in Data Analytics: Transforming Decision-Making, 2024). For example, when a retail company uses AI to pull customer purchase histories, social media interactions, and demographic information, it can better understand consumer behavior and tailor its marketing strategies accordingly.

Identifying Patterns and Trends

After collecting data, AI excels at identifying trends and patterns that might otherwise go unnoticed. Trend analysis through AI involves utilizing sophisticated algorithms capable of processing complex datasets quickly. These algorithms detect subtle changes and emerging patterns, providing organizations with the insight needed for strategic planning. Businesses can anticipate market shifts or organizational changes by recognizing these trends early. For instance, a financial institution can use AI to predict economic downturns based on historical data and adjust its investment strategies proactively. This ability to foresee changes allows companies to stay ahead of competitors and adapt more proficiently to new circumstances (AI in Data Analytics: Transforming Decision-Making, 2024).

Transformation of Raw Data Into Real-Time Reports

AI further simplifies decision-making by transforming raw data into real-time reports. Automated reporting tools powered by AI can analyze vast amounts of data rapidly, generating comprehensive reports that summarize key findings. This capability reduces the workload on human teams, who otherwise would spend considerable time compiling and interpreting data. As a result, employees can focus on higher-level tasks that require creative thinking and problem-solving skills. Moreover, these AI-generated reports maintain consistency and accuracy, minimizing errors that can occur during manual processing (The Use of AI in Real-Time Data Analysis and Decision-Making, 2023). For example, a manufacturing company can harness AI to monitor production metrics and generate daily reports on efficiency and output rates, enabling managers to make informed decisions about resource allocation without delay.

Advantages of Automated Data Analysis and Reporting

A significant advantage of AI in data analytics is its ability to provide actionable insights. By converting analyzed data into practical recommendations, AI supports organizations in implementing strategic initiatives effectively. These insights help businesses align their operations with overarching objectives and drive continuous improvement.

For instance, an e-commerce platform might use AI to analyze customer feedback and sales data, leading to insights on optimizing user interfaces or expanding product lines based on consumer demand. Such valuable input ensures that companies remain adaptable and responsive to evolving market needs.

Incorporating AI into data analysis and reporting processes also offers numerous advantages, including enhanced decision-making capabilities and improved operational efficiency. Real-time tracking emerges as a vital feature, allowing organizations to monitor progress continuously and respond promptly to potential challenges. By keeping track of data as it flows in, businesses can identify bottlenecks in operations and address them before they escalate into larger issues (The Use of AI in Real-Time Data Analysis and Decision-Making, 2023). This proactive approach fosters a dynamic work environment where adjustments can be made on the fly, ultimately driving productivity.

However, transitioning to an AI-supported model for data management requires careful consideration of both technological and human factors. Organizations must ensure data quality and accessibility to maximize the benefits of AI implementations. Investing in data validation, cleaning, and integration ensures that AI solutions have access to accurate and current information, laying the foundation for effective data analysis. Additionally, assembling a skilled team with expertise in data science, machine learning, and computer programming is crucial for managing AI tools and interpreting insights correctly (The Use of AI in Real-Time Data Analysis and Decision-Making, 2023).

Machine Learning in Creative Industries

The integration of machine learning into creative workflows is revolutionizing how we approach content creation and innovation. At the heart of these innovations is generative AI, which plays a pivotal role in brainstorming and idea development. Through models like DALL-E for visual arts or MusicLM for music composition, creators can leverage these tools as digital partners, exploring novel concepts and styles. Generative AI often surprises users with its ability to combine previously unrelated ideas, sparking new directions for creative projects. This collaborative partnership enhances human creativity by expanding the possibilities of imagination while allowing professionals to explore their full potential.

New Ideas

These advanced tools are enhancing creativity without overshadowing human ingenuity, offering new possibilities for professionals across various industries. By providing fresh ideas and overcoming barriers like writer's block, machine learning supports richer creative outputs. In content creation, AI-powered tools such as GPT-4 are capable of drafting articles, generating topic ideas, and even refining language style to align with a specific brand voice. This not only helps individuals to continuously produce engaging content but also allows them to explore a wider range of creative styles and formats.

Design Optimization

Machine learning also excels in design optimization by analyzing vast user feedback to suggest improvements. An example is seen in platforms that use AI algorithms to assess design elements, ensuring designs meet both aesthetic standards and user needs. For instance, a company might employ AI to test different webpage layouts, collecting data on user interaction, which can then be used to refine and enhance the overall user experience. This process leads to innovative solutions that keep pace with changing aesthetics and consumer expectations.

Evaluation of Patterns and Trends

Understanding audience preferences is critical in crafting content strategies that resonate with target demographics. Machine learning evaluates patterns and trends in audience behavior, enabling marketers to devise more effective content strategies. AI tools analyze data from social media interactions, website traffic, and other online activities to identify what type of content attracts viewers. With these insights, professionals can create personalized and targeted content that encourages engagement, enhances loyalty, and ultimately drives success in competitive markets (Integrating AI into Your Creative Workflow: Best Practices for Boosting Productivity and Innovation, n.d.).

Revolutionizing Teamwork Dynamics

Collaborative tools powered by AI have transformed the dynamics of teamwork, especially in remote work settings. Platforms like Slack and Microsoft Teams now integrate AI features to aid in scheduling, managing tasks, and fostering communication. These tools allow team members to collaborate seamlessly despite geographical barriers, encouraging diverse contributions and ideas. Machine learning enables these systems to understand team interactions better, anticipate needs, and even suggest optimal times for meetings based on participants' availability (Generative AI in Content Creation: Revolutionizing Workflows and Boosting Efficiency, 2024).

Ethical Considerations

Ethical considerations remain crucial when integrating AI into creative endeavors. Ensuring that AI-generated content maintains depth and originality requires human oversight. Regular audits and evaluations of AI systems help mitigate potential bias and uphold ethical standards. Striking a balance between AI assistance and human input fosters an environment where both entities contribute meaningfully to the creative process.

Final Insights

AI tools are revolutionizing professional efficiency and collaboration, especially in the field of project management. By automating routine tasks like scheduling and data entry, AI frees time for teams to focus on creative and strategic work. With these systems, resource allocation becomes more precise, helping managers make informed decisions that optimize team efforts and reduce waste. This proactive approach enhances productivity and job satisfaction, illustrating AI's power to transform workplace dynamics positively.

We've also seen how AI's predictive analytics and real-time tracking provide valuable insights, enabling quick adjustments and minimizing risks during projects. These advancements allow professionals not only to stay ahead of challenges but also to navigate their tasks with confidence and ease. For curious newcomers or busy professionals, integrating these AI tools into their routines can simplify complex processes, boost productivity, and open avenues for personal growth. Embracing AI technology offers a practical path toward achieving both professional and personal goals with greater efficiency.

Chapter 4:

Personal Finance and AI

Navigating personal finance has never been more exciting, thanks to the evolving role of AI in this field. From budgeting apps to investment platforms, AI is transforming how we manage our money, making processes smarter and more efficient.

Here, we explore how to leverage AI to enhance financial planning and management, tapping into its vast potential to simplify everyday tasks and offer insights previously reserved for financial experts. As AI becomes an integral part of our lives, understanding its impact on personal finance is crucial for anyone looking to manage their economic well-being.

In this chapter, you'll explore how AI-driven tools can make budgeting a breeze by offering tailored spending analyses and precise financial goal-setting. We'll discuss apps that automatically categorize expenses, saving time and minimizing errors, as well as platforms that provide real-time insights into your financial world.

Discover how AI assists in creating customized investment strategies, employing data-driven approaches to bring clarity and confidence to your investments. Furthermore, learn about the integration of automated bill payments, backed by predictive analysis features, and how they ensure you stay on top of your finances without unnecessary stress.

Finally, the chapter will examine robust security measures provided by AI, protecting your financial data from potential threats while maintaining peace of mind. These topics collectively highlight AI's capabilities, illustrating how it not only enhances financial literacy but also empowers you to take control of your financial future with confidence and ease.

AI in Budgeting and Expense Tracking

Harnessing the power of AI in personal finance has transformed how we approach budgeting, making it more intuitive and effective for individuals from all walks of life. Smart budgeting apps exemplify this shift by analyzing users' spending habits and offering personalized budget suggestions. Unlike traditional methods, these apps leverage advanced algorithms to provide insights tailored to personal behavior, allowing for data-driven financial decision-making that enhances awareness and control over one's economic landscape.

Some examples of AI budgeting and expense-tracking apps include:

- **Mint:** Offers budgeting tools, expense tracking, and financial planning, using AI to provide personalized insights and recommendations.

- **YNAB (You Need A Budget):** Focuses on proactive budgeting and expense tracking, using data analysis to help users manage their finances effectively.

- **PocketGuard:** This app helps users keep track of their spending and budgets while using AI to analyze financial habits and suggest ways to save.

- **Albert:** Combines budgeting and savings features with an AI-driven financial assistant that provides personalized insights and recommendations.

- **Wally:** An expense tracker that uses AI to help users maintain a budget while analyzing spending patterns to offer insights and recommendations.

- **GoodBudget:** A virtual envelope budgeting system that helps users track expenses and manage budgets, using AI for helpful insights on spending habits.

- **Spendee:** Offers collaborative budgeting for groups and tracks expenses while utilizing AI to provide personalized insights and financial advice.

These apps leverage AI to enhance budgeting, track expenses effectively, and provide users with actionable insights for better financial management. Below, we look at some benefits of using AI to help you budget.

Automatic Categorization of Expenses

One of the primary benefits of using AI in budgeting is its ability to automatically categorize expenses. This feature streamlines the process of tracking spending, saving users both time and effort while reducing the chance of manual entry errors. By delegating this often tedious task to an intelligent system, individuals can focus on understanding their spending patterns rather than getting bogged down with details. Such automation not only lifts the burden of meticulous record-keeping but also provides a clear view of where money goes, which is crucial for making informed adjustments to financial habits.

Setting Precise Financial Goals

AI also assists users in setting precise financial goals. These systems evaluate current financial situations and propose strategies to achieve desired objectives, continuously adapting as circumstances change. Whether it's saving for a vacation, building an emergency fund, or planning for retirement, AI-powered apps ensure that users stay aligned with their goals, even when unexpected expenses arise. The flexibility offered by AI allows for proactive planning and increases the likelihood of reaching financial milestones.

Visualization Tools

Visualization tools are another essential component of AI budgeting apps, offering real-time insights through AI-generated reports and graphs. These visual aids demystify complex financial data, making it accessible even to those who might feel overwhelmed by numbers. By transforming raw data into easy-to-understand visuals, AI helps users gain a clearer picture of their financial health, empowering them to make smarter decisions, whether for immediate needs or long-term plans.

Predictive Analysis

Many AI budgeting apps incorporate predictive analysis features, which extend beyond merely tracking past transactions. By forecasting future financial scenarios based on historical data and current trends, these apps offer a glimpse into what lies ahead, enabling users to prepare effectively. Instead of reacting to financial shortfalls or windfalls after they happen, individuals can adjust their budgets proactively, thereby minimizing stress and enhancing control over their finances.

Concerns and Considerations

While the capabilities of AI budgeting apps are impressive, it is important to remember that they are not infallible. Human oversight remains crucial to ensure the accuracy of financial data and address any anomalies that might arise. Regularly reviewing app-generated insights and manually cross-checking figures can help mitigate potential errors and maintain the integrity of your financial planning.

Privacy is another consideration when using AI budgeting apps. Given that these tools handle sensitive financial information, robust security measures are necessary. Users should opt for apps known for their strong security protocols and exercise caution regarding the personal data they share. Being mindful of cybersecurity risks can help protect against breaches and ensure the safety of financial information.

Despite these considerations, the trend of integrating AI into budgeting apps continues to grow, driven by the promise of increased financial literacy and accessibility. As AI evolves, so do these apps, which now often include integration with other financial services such as investment platforms or insurance providers, further simplifying the management of personal finances. These integrations allow users to oversee all aspects of their financial lives from one platform, increasing convenience and efficiency.

Investment Advice Through AI Platforms

AI has emerged as a game-changer for personal finance management, especially when it comes to making investment decisions more accessible to everyone. Some examples of AI investment advice platforms include:

- **Betterment:** An automated investment platform that uses algorithms to provide personalized investment advice and portfolio management based on individual goals.

- **Wealthfront:** Offers automated investment management using AI to create personalized portfolios and provide financial planning advice.

- **Robinhood:** While primarily a trading platform, it uses AI to analyze market trends and provide insights to help users make informed investment decisions.

- **Acorns:** This app helps users invest spare change automatically while using AI to suggest investment strategies based on users' financial goals.

- **SigFig:** Provides personalized investment advice and portfolio management powered by algorithms, optimizing investments based on individual risk tolerance.

- **Zest AI:** While focusing on credit and lending, Zest AI uses machine learning to assess creditworthiness, which can inform investment decisions for institutional investors.

- **Kavout:** An AI-driven investment platform that uses algorithms to analyze stock data and provide investment recommendations and rankings.

These platforms leverage AI technology to analyze data, provide insights, and assist users in making informed investment decisions. By harnessing the power of AI, investors can access tailored guidance that simplifies the traditionally complex landscape of investing in the following ways:

Automated Financial Management

Automated investment platforms, commonly known as robo-advisors, have revolutionized the way people approach investing. These platforms employ sophisticated AI algorithms to manage investments according to user profiles. For instance, they evaluate factors such as age, income, and risk tolerance to construct portfolios designed to optimize returns. This personalized touch ensures that even those with limited investment knowledge can navigate the market with confidence. Robo-advisors often outperform traditional methods by removing human bias and providing consistent strategies that respond dynamically to changing market conditions. This automation not only democratizes access to investment advice but also lowers costs, making professional-grade portfolio management available to a wider audience (Anglen, n.d.).

Customization of Portfolio Strategies

The power of AI extends into creating customized portfolio strategies designed to meet individual financial goals. By analyzing vast datasets—ranging from economic indicators to consumer behavior patterns—AI can craft strategies tailored to specific needs, whether it's saving for retirement or buying a home. This level of customization is achieved thanks to AI's ability to process large volumes of information quickly, enabling real-time adjustments as goals evolve. Investors benefit from having their unique circumstances and aspirations reflected in their investment plans, creating a more meaningful connection between their lives and financial activities (Filipsson, 2024).

Interpreting Market Trends Through Sentiment Analysis

One of AI's standout features is its capacity for sentiment analysis, which helps in interpreting market trends drawn from news articles, social media, and financial reports. Sentiment analysis enables AI systems to gauge the mood of the market and predict potential movements. This capability assists investors in reducing emotional biases that typically cloud human judgment during market volatility. By relying on data-driven insights rather than gut feelings, investors can make informed decisions that align with long-term objectives. While sentiment analysis itself may not require guidelines due to its straightforward implementation, understanding its impact encourages users to trust AI-generated recommendations over instinct-based choices.

Advanced Risk Assessment

AI enhances investment resilience through advanced risk assessment tools. These tools continuously monitor portfolios, offering strategic adjustments to minimize exposure to undue risks. With AI's ability to simulate various market scenarios, investors gain foresight into how different factors might affect their holdings. Stress tests conducted by AI assess the potential impact of extreme events, helping individuals prepare for downturns by adjusting strategies accordingly. This proactive approach to risk management reduces anxiety associated with investing and provides peace of mind, knowing that AI is constantly working to protect and grow assets.

Guidelines

- For automated investment platforms, users should consider defining their financial goals clearly before engaging with a robo-advisor.

- Users of AI-automated investment platforms should regularly review their risk tolerance as life circumstances change, ensuring the platform's recommendations remain aligned with their current situation.

- For those exploring customized portfolio strategies, understanding the underlying data sources and how they influence investment decisions can enhance trust and engagement with the AI-driven process.

- Regularly checking in with the strategy's performance metrics can also provide insights into any required adjustments.

Automated Bill Payments and Reminders

Managing finances can be overwhelming. However, integrating AI into your personal finances can significantly simplify the process and alleviate financial stress. One such area is automating bill payments and reminders through AI, ensuring a hassle-free experience.

Automatic Set-Up of Recurring Transactions

AI-driven systems are designed to facilitate automatic payments by setting up recurring transactions seamlessly. This eliminates the worry of missing due dates, thereby minimizing the risk of incurring late fees and penalties. Consider a scenario where utility bills, subscription services, or even mortgage payments are due every month. With AI, once you set up these recurring payments, the system will automatically handle them for you. This consistency not only ensures timely payments but also allows users to focus on other important aspects of their lives without the constant distraction of manual bill management.

Smart Reminders

Another advantage of using AI in bill management is the smart reminders feature. These AI-enabled notifications alert users about upcoming bills and due dates, facilitating effective financial planning around these schedules. Instead of flipping through calendars or spreadsheets, users receive timely alerts that keep them informed about upcoming financial obligations. This proactive approach empowers individuals to make informed decisions about allocating their resources efficiently, enabling smoother cash flow management throughout the month.

Expense Forecasting

The expense forecasting capabilities of AI add further convenience for users. By analyzing spending patterns and historical data, AI can predict future bills with remarkable accuracy. This predictive insight aids users in crafting more precise budgets. It allows them to allocate funds appropriately and strategically save ahead of time, preventing last-minute scrambles for funds when bills are due. For example, if AI predicts an increase in utility costs during winter months based on past trends, users can adjust their budget accordingly, ensuring they are financially prepared.

Integration With Financial Accounts

Integration with financial accounts is another powerful feature offered by AI, which provides a comprehensive overview of bill management. With all accounts connected, users gain access to a consolidated view of their total outflows. This centralization enhances understanding, making it easier to track and analyze spending behavior. For instance, an AI-integrated platform might offer a dashboard that displays all scheduled payments, recent transactions, and upcoming expenses in one place. This clear, organized presentation of data simplifies decision-making and fosters a deeper comprehension of your financial landscape.

Guidance

To fully leverage the benefits of AI in automating bill payments, it's crucial to choose service providers wisely and ensure full integration with existing financial systems. The setup process involves linking bank accounts and billing information to the AI platform, which then handles the synchronization and automation of transactions. It's essential to periodically review these automated settings to accommodate any changes in personal circumstances or payment schedules.

Furthermore, as AI continues to evolve, the scope of its capabilities is expected to expand, reducing administrative burdens and further enhancing user experiences. However, it's vital to remain vigilant about keeping software updated to benefit from the latest advancements in AI technology, including enhanced data security measures.

Fraud Detection and Security

Safeguarding personal financial information and transactions will bring you security and peace of mind. Advancements in AI have significantly bolstered the security measures around these processes, ensuring a more secure environment for users. We look at some of these advancements below.

Monitoring Financial Transactions in Real Time

One of the most compelling uses of AI lies in its ability to monitor financial transactions in real-time. This powerful feature enables AI systems to detect unusual activities promptly. For instance, if a transaction deviates from a user's typical spending pattern, the AI system can flag it immediately and alert the user, allowing them to take swift action against potential fraud. These real-time alerts offer a practical layer of protection, helping users stay one step ahead of fraudulent activity. Real-time monitoring ensures that any unusual activity is flagged instantly, maintaining a guard over personal finances.

Analyzing User Behavior

Another critical application of AI is in analyzing user behavior. By continuously learning from user interactions, AI can swiftly identify anomalies that might suggest unauthorized access attempts. For instance, if someone tries to access your account from a location you've never visited, AI can predict such discrepancies and trigger necessary alerts or actions. This predictive capability makes AI an indispensable ally in preempting unauthorized access, reinforcing the security framework that many users now depend upon.

Two-Factor Authentication

The introduction of AI-driven two-factor authentication is another leap forward in online transaction safety. This multifaceted verification method typically involves confirming a user's identity by sending a unique code to a registered device or email before granting access. AI enhances this process by analyzing patterns and adapting to irregularities. For example, if you're logging in from a new device, AI can request additional verification steps, thus adding an extra layer of security. This ensures that even if login credentials are compromised, unauthorized access remains thwarted, shielding sensitive financial data from potential breaches.

Streamlining and Simplification of Reporting

When it comes to reporting suspicious activities, AI streamlines and simplifies the often cumbersome process. Traditionally, reporting fraud required multiple steps, which could delay responses and complicate resolutions. However, with AI, users benefit from automated procedures that collect and analyze necessary information quickly. Suppose there's a need to report a dubious transaction; AI systems can autonomously gather relevant details and present them clearly, enabling quicker response and recovery. Thus, AI not only aids in identifying threats but also accelerates the entire resolution process, minimizing potential damage and distress for users. Streamlined fraud reporting provides clear protocols for action as soon as a threat is identified, reducing reaction time and optimizing recovery efforts.

Final Insights

AI in financial planning is transforming the way we handle our money. This chapter has showcased several practical applications of AI, making complex tasks like budgeting, investment, and bill management more manageable. Through smart budgeting apps, personalized financial suggestions are now at our fingertips. By automating tasks such as expense tracking and payment scheduling, AI frees up mental space for what truly matters. These tools not only streamline daily tasks but also provide a clearer picture of our financial health, enabling smarter decisions. The power of AI doesn't stop at personal finance—it extends into investments, offering tailored guidance through robo-advisors that simplify investing for everyone.

As technology evolves, the integration of AI into financial management will continue to grow, offering even more ways to enhance productivity and security. While these advancements may seem overwhelming, they promise increased financial literacy and control. AI keeps us informed and prepared by predicting financial scenarios and monitoring transactions for potential fraud. For those seeking personal growth or efficient time management, adopting AI can lead to significant life improvements. Whether you're a busy professional or someone looking to leverage tech for self-improvement, AI provides the tools needed to navigate your financial journey with confidence and ease.

Chapter 5:

AI in Health and Well-Being

AI's impact on health and well-being is reshaping how we approach our fitness journeys, making personalization an exciting new norm. With its ability to intuitively assess personal needs and adapt to our unique lifestyles, AI offers a compelling alternative to one-size-fits-all solutions in both exercise and nutrition.

Now your workout plan can be dynamically adjusted based on your sleep patterns or daily energy levels, ensuring every session leaves you feeling accomplished rather than overextended. Not only does this technology improve the effectiveness of regimens but also keeps us more invested, turning mundane routines into engaging experiences tailored just for us. Meanwhile, AI's applications aren't limited to exercise alone—it plays a crucial role in guiding dietary choices too.

By understanding individual calorie needs and identifying food sensitivities, AI assists in crafting meal plans that align with our wellness goals, be it losing weight, building muscle, or simply maintaining a balanced lifestyle. The seamless integration of this kind of precision into daily routines empowers us to make smarter choices.

Below, we look at various AI-driven tools that can enhance our health practices. This chapter explores AI-powered fitness apps that design personalized workout plans and nutrition tracking systems offering bespoke dietary guidance. Wearable technology like fitness trackers exemplifies another frontier where AI significantly enhances user experience. These devices gather continuous data on physical activity and vitals, offering real-time feedback that drives better health outcomes.

Furthermore, AI extends its benefits by linking individuals with like-minded community members through digital platforms, bolstering motivation via shared challenges and victories. Social connectivity within these applications turns exercises into communal activities, enriching personal motivation and accountability. The chapter also highlights AI's adaptability in adjusting fitness plans instantaneously, catering to changing conditions such as fatigue or insufficient rest. By exploring these advancements, readers will gain insight into how AI simplifies achieving wellness objectives, reducing guesswork while maximizing efficiency. This journey through AI's roles showcases how technology not only brings accessibility and effectiveness but also transforms our health pursuits into rewarding, sustainable adventures.

AI-Powered Fitness and Nutrition Apps

In recent years, the integration of AI into health and well-being has greatly increased fitness accessibility and effectiveness. By simplifying fitness personalization and improving access through advanced technology, AI is transforming traditional approaches to health and wellness. It eliminates much of the guesswork involved in personal fitness endeavors, replacing it with informed guidance that evolves as you tick off your health and fitness goals. As AI becomes more integrated into daily life, its potential to facilitate healthier lifestyles becomes even more apparent. Individuals can now tailor their wellness plans to reflect precise needs and preferences, resulting in a more sustainable and enjoyable path to achieving their health goals. We look at how AI helps with fitness and nutrition below.

Personalized Workout Regimens

One of its most compelling features is the ability to personalize workout regimens by analyzing user data. This personalized approach tailor exercises to fit each individual's goals, preferences, and lifestyle, leading to higher chances of achieving desired results. Unlike generic workout programs, AI-driven plans consider real-time data such as workout performance, sleep patterns, and physical readiness, creating a dynamic regimen that adapts to the user's progress and condition (The AI Revolution in Wellness: How Personalised Health Plans Are Getting Smarter, 2025).

AI not only customizes these workout routines but also makes them more engaging and effective. Users who engage with AI-guided exercise programs often find themselves more motivated due to the personalized feedback they receive. This level of customization caters to the specific needs of each individual, which enhances both the effectiveness of the workout and the likelihood of adherence over time. Personalized plans are proven to boost user engagement, keeping followers motivated as they witness tangible improvements in their fitness journey.

AI-Powered Nutrition Tracking Apps

Nutrition plays a critical role in overall health and fitness. AI-powered nutrition tracking apps have revolutionized dietary planning by offering tailored advice based on user-specific data. These applications analyze factors like calorie intake, food sensitivities, and activity levels, providing meal recommendations that align with personal goals such as weight management, muscle gain, or energy balance. Such targeted dietary suggestions help users make informed choices about their eating habits, supporting long-term health and wellness objectives. By considering individual dietary needs, AI empowers users to stay on track with healthier options that complement their fitness efforts.

Wearable Technology

Wearable technology is another domain where AI excels, integrating seamlessly into users' daily activities. Devices like fitness trackers and smartwatches continuously collect data on metrics such as heart rate, steps taken, and calories burned. This constant flow of information enables AI systems to provide actionable feedback in real-time, promoting improved physical performance and accountability. Wearables offer users an insightful glance at their health metrics, encouraging consistent activity monitoring and adjustment. The value lies in how these devices assist individuals in understanding their body's responses to different activities, ultimately shaping a more effective path toward health improvement (Fabbrizio et al., 2023).

Social Features and Community Support

Beyond individualized feedback, AI-driven platforms often include social features that leverage community support to enhance motivation. Apps incorporating these elements create virtual spaces for users to engage in shared challenges, fostering a sense of camaraderie and competition. This social interaction can significantly boost motivation levels, urging users to push beyond their limits in pursuit of communal goals. Engaging with others on similar journeys can inspire accountability and drive, making AI-powered fitness solutions more than just tools—they become part of a supportive network of wellness enthusiasts.

Real-Time Adjustments

AI's adaptability extends to real-time adjustments based on immediate feedback. If a user logs insufficient sleep or displays signs of fatigue, for instance, the system might suggest modifying the day's workout intensity. These adjustments ensure that users avoid overtraining while still maintaining a productive exercise regime. AI's capability to react quickly to changing conditions is invaluable, allowing individuals to remain proactive about their health without risking injury or burnout.

Healthcare Scheduling and Reminders

AI is revolutionizing healthcare by streamlining logistics to improve patient management. Let's look at how it's done.

Automated Appointment Scheduling

One of the most significant contributions of AI in this field is automating appointment scheduling, a tool that drastically minimizes wait times and ensures easy access to medical services. For instance, if you wake up one morning feeling under the weather; instead of spending hours trying to get through to a clinic or browsing dozens of web pages, an AI system quickly finds suitable slots across various healthcare providers, comparing availability and even your personal preferences for meeting times.

By eliminating back-and-forth negotiations and manual coordination, these systems free up human staff time, reduce frustration, and immediately book appointments when cancellations occur, enhancing overall efficiency and patient satisfaction.

Medication Reminders

AI makes life simpler and safer with medication reminders. For many, especially those managing chronic conditions, keeping track of prescriptions is a daily challenge. AI-based apps or devices send timely alerts to ensure patients take their medications as prescribed. This not only helps maintain treatment efficacy but significantly reduces risks associated with missed doses, like worsening health conditions or hospitalizations. Such tools can also detect inconsistencies or potential drug interactions, prompting users to consult their healthcare provider. Thus, AI turns what might be a complex schedule into an easily manageable routine, increasing adherence and improving health outcomes.

Telehealth

The integration of telehealth is another transformative application of AI. It breaks down geographical barriers, offering remote consultations and follow-up care. AI enhances these virtual visits, allowing healthcare providers to gather and analyze data effectively before, during, or after sessions. This leads to more informed advice and decision-making. Additionally, by providing a platform accessible from anywhere, patients experience a level of convenience that encourages them to attend regular check-ups and follow-ups, promoting better long-term health maintenance.

Organization of Patient Data

Beyond individual interactions, AI's role in organizing massive volumes of patient data is invaluable for healthcare practitioners. In an era where information is abundant, sifting through electronic medical records, test results, and historical data to make informed decisions can be overwhelming. AI-driven systems swiftly organize and analyze this data, offering insights that support clinicians in crafting targeted treatment plans. Not only does this help in diagnosing conditions more accurately, but it also enables predictive analytics that anticipate health events, further empowering preventive measures. By alleviating the analytical burden on healthcare professionals, AI ensures they have more time and mental space to focus on patient care and personalized treatments.

Facilitating Communication in Healthcare

AI plays a crucial role in enhancing communication between different segments of the healthcare system. It links primary care physicians with specialists, pharmacists, and caregivers seamlessly. When a patient needs a referral or transition between care levels, AI facilitates swift and accurate data transfer, ensuring continuity of care. Through intelligent algorithms, these systems highlight relevant information, flag urgent cases, and update all parties involved without delay, thereby creating an interconnected network that prioritizes patient well-being over administrative hurdles.

Cost Effective

Another essential benefit of utilizing AI in healthcare logistics is cost-effectiveness. With streamlined operations, hospitals and clinics reduce overhead costs while maximizing resource usage. Automated scheduling decreases no-show rates, leading to optimal use of clinical time and space. Data-driven decision-making diminishes unnecessary tests or procedures, focusing instead on effective, evidence-based interventions. Consequently, healthcare providers offer high-quality care at more competitive prices, helping both themselves and their patients.

Telemedicine Advancements

AI is revolutionizing remote medical consultations and care delivery, breaking down long-standing barriers to healthcare access. Here, we look at the AI-fueled telemedicine advancements at the forefront of modern healthcare practice.

Virtual Consultations

Virtual consultations, powered by AI technology enable patients to connect with healthcare providers from virtually anywhere, making medical advice more accessible than ever before. This advancement is particularly significant for people living in remote or underserved areas where traditional healthcare infrastructure might be limited. By leveraging AI, virtual consultations bypass geographical constraints, ensuring that everyone has the opportunity to receive expert medical guidance.

AI Diagnostic Tools

AI diagnostic tools enhance these virtual interactions by improving the accuracy of condition assessments during telemedicine appointments. Traditionally, an accurate diagnosis heavily relied on in-person evaluations and tests. However, AI algorithms can now analyze symptoms, medical history, and even real-time data from wearable devices to assist healthcare professionals in diagnosing conditions more precisely from afar. This increases the reliability of telemedicine consultations and speeds up the process of identifying and addressing health issues, which is crucial for effective treatment outcomes.

AI Support in Follow-Up Care

AI plays a pivotal role in supporting follow-up care through timely reminders. These intelligent systems ensure continuity by sending alerts for medication schedules, upcoming check-ups, and lifestyle recommendations. Such reminders are vital in maintaining consistent patient engagement, as they help individuals adhere to their prescribed treatment plans and monitor their recovery progress. This approach improves the overall quality of care received and encourages a proactive attitude toward personal health management.

Crisis Management

Crisis management capabilities offered by AI in remote healthcare further bolster its effectiveness. During emergencies, AI systems can prioritize urgent needs, optimizing the allocation of healthcare resources. For instance, predictive analytics can identify patterns or trends in patient data that may indicate an impending crisis, such as a heart attack or diabetic episode. By quickly flagging these potential emergencies, AI enables healthcare providers to take immediate action, allocating necessary resources and attention precisely where they're needed the most. This capability minimizes risks and enhances patient safety, especially in time-sensitive situations.

Benefits

The integration of AI in remote healthcare presents numerous benefits beyond individual patient interactions.

- It allows healthcare systems to operate more efficiently by managing large volumes of data and streamlining processes.

- Remote consultations supported by AI reduce the load on physical healthcare facilities, freeing up resources to attend to more critical cases.

- AI-driven insights derived from aggregated patient data can lead to better public health strategies and more informed decision-making at multiple levels of the healthcare system.

Ethical Considerations

Despite these advancements, there remain challenges that must be addressed to fully realize the potential of AI in remote healthcare. Ethical considerations, privacy concerns, and the need for robust regulatory frameworks are critical aspects that require ongoing attention. Ensuring fairness, safety, and accountability in AI applications is paramount to building trust and maximizing their positive impact on society.

Mental Health Support Through AI

In recent years, the integration of AI into mental health care has opened up new avenues for support and management. For many individuals interested in personal development, AI offers practical solutions that integrate seamlessly into daily life. With AI-enabled mental health applications, users can access support at any time, fitting in moments of mindfulness or reflection amidst hectic schedules. This flexibility not only aids in stress reduction but also enhances overall productivity by promoting a balanced lifestyle. Here we look at how AI facilitates mental health support.

AI Chatbots

AI chatbots are revolutionizing immediate mental health assistance by offering rapid, confidential support. They engage users in conversations that are tailored to their individual emotional needs, creating a space where people can explore coping strategies without fear or hesitation. The convenience and anonymity provided by AI chatbots make them an ideal first step for those who may feel apprehensive about seeking traditional therapy. These digital companions are equipped to respond in real-time, offering reassurance and guidance that can alleviate anxiety and stress.

AI Mood-Tracking Applications

AI-powered mood-tracking applications have become instrumental tools for individuals managing their mental health. By consistently monitoring emotional patterns, these apps provide users with a comprehensive overview of their mental state over time. This data is invaluable during therapy sessions, as it offers insights that might not be readily apparent through conversation alone. For instance, noticing recurring periods of low mood can help therapists identify potential triggers and devise more effective treatment plans. Such insights empower both therapists and users to understand underlying issues better, thereby enhancing the overall effectiveness of therapy (Haque & Rubya, 2023).

Recommending Therapeutic Exercises

Another remarkable contribution of AI to mental health is through the recommendation of therapeutic exercises. These exercises are specifically designed to enhance personal mental well-being, encouraging users to take active steps toward self-care. Whether it's guided mindfulness sessions or interactive cognitive-behavioral therapy exercises, AI tailors these recommendations to fit individual needs, ensuring users engage with activities that resonate with them. This personalization not only increases engagement but also helps users develop sustainable practices for maintaining mental health over the long term.

Identifying Signs of Distress

AI's ability to identify signs of distress in users is another significant advancement. By analyzing patterns in communication and behavior, AI systems can detect subtle indicators of increased risk levels, enabling timely crisis intervention. This feature is particularly beneficial for vulnerable individuals who might not actively reach out for help. Early detection allows for immediate response measures, which can drastically reduce the likelihood of harm. It acts as a safety net, providing users with extra security and peace of mind knowing that help is always within reach when needed.

Confidentiality

Confidentiality remains a cornerstone in the success of AI in mental health management. Users appreciate the discretion offered by AI-driven tools, allowing them to explore personal topics without judgment. This sense of privacy encourages more open communication about feelings and experiences, which can lead to more accurate assessments and interventions. Furthermore, the non-judgmental nature of AI ensures that all interactions are met with empathy, fostering a supportive environment conducive to healing and growth.

Looking ahead, the continuous evolution of AI in mental health care highlights the need for ethical implementation and user-centric design. While the benefits are substantial, it is crucial to address potential challenges such as privacy concerns, bias mitigation, and ensuring equitable access for all users. As this technology advances, establishing clear guidelines and standards will be imperative to maintain trust and efficacy in AI-based mental health solutions (Olawade et al., 2024).

Final Insights

As we reflect, it's clear how AI is reshaping our approach to health and wellness with its innovative applications. From personalized fitness routines to tailored nutrition advice, these AI-driven solutions are making it easier for everyone to embark on a healthier lifestyle. They provide practical tools that cater to individual needs, ensuring that achieving fitness goals becomes a more achievable endeavor.

Such technology enhances personal motivation and encourages a sense of community through shared challenges and progress reports. This transformation means that wellness isn't a solitary endeavor; it's one where AI acts as a supportive companion, offering guidance and encouragement every step of the way.

Moreover, wearable technology has seamlessly integrated into our daily lives, providing real-time data that empowers us to make informed decisions about our health. These gadgets aren't just about tracking numbers—they're about understanding your body better and adapting to its unique requirements.

Additionally, the social features present in many AI-powered apps have built virtual communities that keep individuals connected and motivated. In merging technology with camaraderie, AI is crafting a wellness landscape where each person can thrive. It promises a future where maintaining good health is convenient, engaging, and above all, within reach for everyone looking to improve their well-being with the help of technology.

Chapter 6:

AI in Learning and Education

AI is reshaping the educational landscape by integrating innovative tools into learning. It offers fresh perspectives on how education can be personalized to fit each learner's unique needs. The traditional one-size-fits-all approach is gradually giving way to more individualized experiences, thanks to AI's capacity to analyze and respond to diverse student requirements in real-time. As educational practices evolve, the potential for AI-driven customization becomes a topic of great interest for educators, students, and institutions alike. This transformation highlights the dynamic relationship between technology and education and sets the stage for a future where learning is an engaging and tailored experience.

Here, we'll consider how AI enhances educational experiences through personalized learning platforms. We'll explore adaptive learning algorithms that shape lessons based on student performance, ensuring neither boredom nor frustration is part of the learning journey. The discussion will then extend to AI's role in crafting individualized lesson plans that cater to distinct educational backgrounds and preferences.

Additionally, you'll discover how AI contributes valuable insights to educators, aiding them in refining instructional strategies and improving classroom effectiveness. We'll also touch upon the influence of gamification, which merges fun with learning to sustain motivation and participation. By understanding these AI-powered innovations, readers will grasp the transformative potential AI holds for creating a more personalized and effective educational environment.

Personalized Learning Platforms

AI is transforming the educational sector, particularly through personalized learning platforms. These platforms harness AI to adapt educational experiences to the distinctive needs of each student, moving away from traditional, uniform teaching methods. AI in learning offers systemic benefits as well. Educational institutions equipped with AI technologies can transcend conventional teaching methods, adopting more nuanced and flexible approaches that account for each learner's strengths, weaknesses, and interests.

Such advancements reflect a paradigm shift in education, where the focus shifts from rote memorization to fostering critical thinking and creativity through personalized pathways. Below, we look at some of the features of these AI-powered personalized learning platforms.

Adaptive Learning Algorithms

Adaptive learning algorithms are at the core of these personalized learning platforms. They evaluate a student's performance in real-time, adjusting the difficulty and content of lessons based on their progress. This dynamic adjustment ensures that learners are neither overwhelmed by challenges nor bored with tasks that are too easy. For instance, platforms like DreamBox employ such algorithms to monitor students' responses and tailor the complexity of math problems accordingly. This customization enables students to learn at their own pace, catering to their unique learning curves and facilitating more effective knowledge retention (Echeverry, 2024).

Individual Lesson Plans

AI also plays a crucial role in developing individualized lesson plans. By analyzing vast amounts of student data, AI systems can curate learning resources that suit a variety of educational backgrounds and learning styles. This personalization extends to offering alternative materials for students who struggle with traditional textbooks or find certain explanations ineffective. Such tailored lesson plans empower educators to address diverse classroom needs without being bogged down by one-size-fits-all solutions. According to McKinsey research, personalized learning can enhance student outcomes by up to 30%, underscoring the significant impact of AI-driven customization on educational success (Manoharan, 2024).

The Educational Potential of Data Analysis

AI's ability to perform data analysis provides educators with critical insights into student weaknesses. Teachers can identify areas where students consistently underperform and adjust the curriculum accordingly, focusing efforts where they are most needed. By leveraging these insights, educators can refine instructional strategies, further personalizing the educational experience to optimize learning outcomes. This informed approach fosters an environment where students receive targeted support, ultimately improving both individual performance and overall classroom effectiveness.

Gamification

An equally compelling feature of AI in education is its incorporation of gamification. Integrating game-like elements into learning environments increases motivation and engagement by presenting students with interactive challenges tailored to their skill levels. Platforms such as Duolingo exemplify this approach by using AI to devise personalized language exercises that keep learners engaged and motivated. This method not only makes learning fun but also encourages consistent participation, which is crucial for continually honing skills. Gamified learning has the potential to increase student engagement by up to 60%, showcasing its powerful influence on maintaining learner interest (Le, 2024).

Furthermore, gamification serves as a bridge between learning and entertainment, turning mundane educational tasks into captivating activities. By rewarding achievements and milestones with badges or points, these educational games reinforce positive behaviors, driving students to master new concepts enthusiastically. Tailored challenges that align with a student's current abilities ensure that progress feels satisfying rather than frustrating, promoting a positive learning experience.

Guidance

Amidst these advancements, it is essential to remember that while AI offers remarkable opportunities, integration should be approached with care. Educators must balance technological innovation with human oversight, ensuring AI tools complement rather than replace the intuitive and empathetic aspects of teaching. The ultimate goal is to create a harmonious synergy between AI capabilities and human expertise, optimizing educational experiences for diverse learners.

AI Tutors and Study Aids

AI-driven tutoring systems are transforming educational experiences, extending learning beyond the traditional classroom. These systems provide unique advantages and cater to the varying needs of learners by offering flexible, personalized support. AI-driven tutoring systems are also hailed for their wide reach and scalability, making high-quality education accessible to students regardless of geographic location or financial limitations. Whether it's a student living in a rural area or someone in an urban setting, all they need is an internet connection to access valuable educational resources. This democratization of education ensures every student has equal opportunities to learn and grow.

We explore some of the main advantages of AI tutors and study aids below.

24/7 Availability

One of the most significant benefits of AI tutoring is its 24/7 availability. Unlike traditional tutors who may have limited hours, AI tutors can assist students at any time of day or night. This continuous accessibility allows students to incorporate learning into their schedules more easily, whether they're early risers or night owls. For busy professionals or parents balancing multiple responsibilities, this flexibility means educational advancement doesn't have to take a back seat. By integrating learning into their lives when convenient, users can enjoy a more seamless experience, enhancing their educational journey without disrupting daily routines (The Impact of Artificial Intelligence on Virtual Tutoring, n.d.).

Interactive Study Aids

Interactive study aids are another characteristic of AI tutors that captivate students' attention. Through simulations and other engaging formats, these tools present complex concepts in an understandable way, encouraging deeper comprehension and knowledge retention. Simulations create immersive environments where students can experiment with materials and see the immediate effects of their decisions, making lessons vivid and memorable. Science students might interact with virtual labs that recreate real-world scientific experiments, while those studying history could explore interactive timelines that bring past events to life. These features not only enrich the learning experience but also encourage active participation, making it easier for students to grasp challenging subjects and ideas.

Tailored Assistance

Tailored assistance is a defining feature of AI tutoring systems. These systems assess individual interactions to provide specific feedback, ensuring each student receives personalized guidance. Imagine tackling a math problem and receiving instant feedback that helps you understand your mistake and solve it correctly on your next attempt. This level of support mimics one-on-one attention from a human tutor and fosters a supportive learning environment, ultimately boosting confidence. By adapting to each student's pace, approach, and learning style, AI tutors cater to diverse needs, helping learners overcome obstacles and achieve goals efficiently (AI for Tutoring: Real-Time Support and Feedback, 2024).

Tracking Progress

AI-powered tools also excel in tracking progress by compiling comprehensive data on student performance. By analyzing this data, educators and learners gain insights into individual strengths and weaknesses, facilitating targeted improvement efforts. Detailed reports allow students to monitor their progress over time, set achievable goals, and celebrate milestones. Educators benefit from this data as well, using it to adjust instructional strategies to better meet students' needs. For instance, if a student struggles with a particular topic, teachers can provide additional resources or practice exercises to address these gaps proactively. This informed approach leads to more efficient learning paths and improved outcomes.

Language Learning Through AI

The intersection of AI and language learning presents remarkable opportunities for personalized education. AI has revolutionized language acquisition by providing real-time, individualized feedback, enhancing vocabulary retention, and immersing learners in cultural nuances.

Conversational Practice via App

One of the standout features of AI in language learning is its ability to offer conversational practice through applications that provide immediate feedback on pronunciation and grammar. For instance, an AI tutor can listen to your speech in real-time, identifying pronunciation issues and correcting grammatical errors instantly. This level of interaction is vital for learners who lack access to native speakers or traditional language courses. Applications such as Duolingo enable learners to improve their language skills through interactive exercises with real-time feedback. This feature aids learners in refining pronunciation and grammar, crucial elements for effective communication.

The adaptive nature of AI ensures that learners receive targeted assistance, enabling them to improve their speaking accuracy and fluency over time. For example, platforms powered by machine learning can simulate conversations in different dialects, allowing students to hone their listening and speaking skills across various accents. By doing so, these AI-driven tools not only enhance pronunciation competencies but also broaden users' overall language proficiency (Girimonte, 2024).

Vocabulary Enhancement

AI improves language learning through vocabulary enhancement methods that combine contextual learning, interactive quizzes, and spaced repetition. These tools make memorizing new words more effective by presenting them in relevant contexts, which helps with long-term retention. Instead of relying solely on rote memorization, learners are immersed in environments where new terms naturally occur, making it easier to grasp meaning and usage. Interactive quizzes keep the process engaging, encouraging learners to actively participate in their education. Spaced repetition, an evidence-based technique for improving recall, schedules review sessions based on how well a learner remembers each word. This strategic approach ensures that learners solidify their understanding of vocabulary over time (Ahmad, 2024).

Vocabulary enhancement tools offered by AI provide interactive quizzes and contextual learning, helping with memorization and retention. These tools use spaced repetition techniques to ensure that learners frequently review vocabulary at intervals optimized for memory retention. An example is Quizlet, which uses AI algorithms to adapt lessons according to the learner's progress, facilitating a deeper understanding of new words.

Cultural Contextualization

Language and culture are interconnected; understanding one without the other limits effective communication. AI facilitates this integration by including idiomatic expressions and cultural nuances within lessons, helping learners navigate complex social interactions. Consider an AI application that teaches Spanish by weaving in common sayings from different Spanish-speaking regions or using local news articles for reading comprehension exercises. By exposing students to authentic content, AI enables a richer learning experience that transcends basic language mechanics. This cultural immersion is invaluable as it equips learners with the knowledge to engage respectfully and effectively in multilingual environments.

Cultural contextualization also enriches communication skills by integrating expressions that are natural to native speakers and cultural nuances into the learning process. Language learning platforms that embed cultural lessons help learners understand and appreciate the context in which languages are used, making their communication more authentic and nuanced. This holistic approach to language learning ensures learners not only speak a language but also comprehend its cultural backdrop.

AI-Driven Assessments

To maintain continuous engagement and track progress, AI-driven assessments play a vital role in evaluating proficiency levels and tailoring educational plans accordingly. These assessments analyze performances regularly, adjusting lesson difficulty and focus areas based on individual needs. As learners advance, their goals evolve, necessitating a personalized plan that accommodates these changes. For example, once a student masters basic vocabulary, the system may introduce complex sentence structures or advanced grammatical concepts to challenge and motivate further development. By ensuring that educational experiences remain aligned with personal growth, AI fosters a seamless transition between skill levels, preventing disengagement and plateauing.

AI-driven assessment tools regularly evaluate proficiency levels, allowing for the adjustment of learning plans for continuous engagement and improvement. Through data analysis, educators and learners can track progress and identify areas for further development. Adaptive learning platforms such as Eduaide.AI provide continuous assessments that guide learners in focusing their efforts where needed, ensuring steady advancement in skill proficiency (Poth, 2023).

AI-Supported Skill Development

Skill assessment tools powered by AI are transforming the way individuals approach learning new skills. Below, we explore how they are doing this.

Intelligent Algorithms

By utilizing intelligent algorithms, these tools can effectively evaluate a learner's strengths and weaknesses, offering immediate insights that traditional methods might overlook. This targeted approach to learning ensures that individuals concentrate on areas that need improvement, optimizing their learning process. For example, AI-driven platforms like iMocha allow users to undertake assessments that identify skill gaps, enabling them to focus on strengthening those areas (What Are the AI Tools for Career Development Programs in 2025?, 2024). Such tools not only save time but also make learning more efficient and personalized.

Specialized Content and Learning Materials

AI curates specialized content and learning materials tailored to individual preferences, which significantly boosts engagement and motivation. AI has several applications that know your preferred learning style—be it visual, auditory, or kinesthetic—and adjust content delivery accordingly. Platforms like LinkedIn Learning leverage AI to recommend courses aligned with personal interests and career goals, ensuring relevance and fostering continuous engagement (What Are the AI Tools for Career Development Programs in 2025?, 2024). By aligning educational content with a learner's unique preferences, AI maintains a high level of motivation, crucial for effective skill acquisition.

Virtual Mentorship

Virtual mentorship is another area where AI is making a notable impact. With virtual mentorship programs, learners have access to expert guidance and accountability without the constraints of geographic location. These programs connect learners with mentors who can provide valuable insights and support. Through AI-mediated interactions, individuals receive timely feedback and advice, which greatly enhances the learning experience. Services like BetterUp and CoachHub offer personalized coaching experiences by connecting learners with certified coaches worldwide, creating a rich environment for personal growth and learning (What Are the AI Tools for Career Development Programs in 2025?, 2024).

AI-Supported Project-Based Learning

Project-based learning, supported by AI, plays a significant role in skill development. By engaging learners in real-world projects, this method encourages the practical application of acquired knowledge, thereby boosting confidence and competence. AI tools can assist in forming collaborative teams, managing workflow, and providing feedback, thus making project-based learning more dynamic and effective. As learners work on real-world challenges, they naturally enhance their problem-solving skills, creativity, and ability to work within a team. This experiential learning approach is invaluable, as it not only improves practical skills but also prepares individuals for professional environments where collaboration and innovation are key.

Final Insights

We've explored how AI-driven tools are reshaping educational experiences, particularly through personalized learning platforms. These tools tailor educational content to the unique needs of each student, ensuring that learning is paced to match individual abilities. By using adaptive algorithms, AI customizes lesson plans and provides vital insights into areas where students may need extra help. This nurturing environment not only bolsters students' confidence but also enhances their overall learning journey. Moreover, by incorporating elements like gamification, AI makes education engaging and fun, encouraging consistent participation and keeping learners motivated.

These advanced tools are revolutionizing traditional teaching methods, providing educators with the flexibility to personalize instruction and optimize outcomes for diverse groups of learners. However, it's important to balance these innovations with human insight, ensuring that AI serves as an aid rather than a replacement for the intuitive aspects of teaching. By harmoniously blending technology with human expertise, we can create an enriching educational sector that equips both students and educators to thrive.

Chapter 7:

Travel and Transportation With AI

Navigating the world of travel and transportation has never been more exciting, thanks to the power of artificial intelligence. AI is revolutionizing how we plan trips and manage transportation, offering unprecedented levels of convenience and personalization for travelers of all kinds. Now you can craft a perfectly tailored itinerary that aligns seamlessly with your personal preferences and lifestyle, or have access to dynamic travel plans that adapt in real-time, accommodating everything from sudden weather changes to unexpected delays. Through its transformative capabilities, AI ensures that every journey becomes not only manageable but also a truly memorable experience, allowing you to focus on exploring and enjoying new destinations.

In this chapter, we'll dive into the various ways AI simplifies travel planning and transport management. You'll discover how AI can create personalized itineraries, making it easier than ever to tailor your travel experiences to your unique tastes and interests. We'll explore the magic behind AI-driven adaptability, which keeps your plans flexible and resilient in the face of unforeseen events.

Additionally, we'll examine collaborative tools that streamline group travel planning, ensuring harmonious adventures with family and friends. As you read on, you'll also learn about AI's role in optimizing travel budgets, helping you make the most of your resources without sacrificing quality. Each section of this chapter will reveal practical applications of AI technologies that enhance productivity, simplify complexities, and enrich your travel journeys, ultimately empowering you to leverage AI's full potential for a smoother, smarter way of moving across the globe.

AI in Trip Planning and Itineraries

AI has emerged as a transformative force, reshaping how we approach trip planning and creating tailored itineraries. By leveraging AI technologies, travelers can now enjoy a more personalized and streamlined experience, making journey preparation less daunting and more enjoyable.

Personalized Recommendations

One of the primary benefits of integrating AI into travel planning is its ability to offer personalized recommendations. Through advanced algorithms that analyze user preferences and past behavior, AI-powered travel advisors can craft itineraries that align with individual interests. For example, AI tools quickly become aware of your likes and dislikes, such as a love for hiking or sampling local cuisines, offering you a list of must-visit trails or top-rated eateries at your destination. Such personalized touches ensure each trip aligns with the traveler's unique style and desires, enriching the overall journey. This personalization elevates the travel experience from sightseeing to a deeply engaging exploration tailored just for you (Venkatesh, 2024).

Adaptability

AI-driven itineraries excel in their adaptability. Traditional static itineraries often fall short when faced with unexpected changes like sudden weather shifts or local event cancellations. However, AI-infused planning tools dynamically adjust plans in real-time. For instance, if rain is expected during a planned outdoor activity, the itinerary will seamlessly rearrange to accommodate indoor alternatives or reschedule the activity for another day. This flexibility transforms potential disruptions into opportunities for spontaneity and discovery, ensuring travelers are not left scrambling when plans go awry (Smart Travel Planner: How AI is Revolutionizing Travel Planning, 2024).

Collaborative AI Tools

When planning trips with friends or family, balancing everyone's preferences can become challenging. Here, collaborative AI tools prove invaluable by facilitating group trip planning. These tools aggregate input from all participants, weighing everyone's suggestions and preferences to create a cohesive plan that satisfies the entire group. Whether coordinating flight times, deciding on shared accommodations, or scheduling activities that appeal to diverse interests, these AI tools streamline decision-making processes while ensuring all voices are heard. This collaborative functionality fosters a harmonious travel experience, reducing conflicts and enhancing enjoyment (Venkatesh, 2024).

Managing Travel Expenses

Managing travel expenses is another crucial aspect where AI proves beneficial. Cost estimation powered by AI helps optimize spending by analyzing various financial factors, such as accommodation prices, dining costs, and activity fees. By highlighting peak and off-peak pricing trends, AI assists travelers in crafting an itinerary that fits comfortably within their budget without compromising on quality. Travelers can also receive alerts about discounted deals and special offers relevant to their destinations, allowing them to make cost-effective decisions. This budgeting support ensures resources are allocated wisely, ultimately leading to a more satisfying and stress-free travel experience (Smart Travel Planner: How AI is Revolutionizing Travel Planning, 2024).

Guidelines

To fully leverage these AI capabilities, guidelines can enhance the planning process.

- It's important to keep your itinerary flexible and open to adjustments. Embrace changes and let the AI suggest alternatives during unforeseen events, which enriches your journey with unexpected but rewarding experiences.

- When using collaborative planning tools, engage all members of your travel party in the planning phase to gather comprehensive input. Establishing clear communication early mitigates misunderstandings and ensures the final plan aligns with everyone's expectations.

- During the cost estimation and budgeting stage, provide detailed insights into your spending limits and preferences to help the AI generate the most accurate suggestions.

- Regularly review your itinerary to ensure it remains aligned with any budgetary adjustments or newfound preferences.

Smart Navigation and Traffic Management

By leveraging AI technology, we have the potential to transform how we travel, making it more efficient and less stressful. Here we look at the key components of this transformation.

Real-Time Traffic Data

With AI, navigation systems provide up-to-date guidance by continuously analyzing live traffic feeds from various sources such as GPS devices, cameras, and road sensors. This ensures that drivers receive the most current information on traffic conditions at any given moment, allowing them to alter their routes accordingly.

Real-time data collection is also about promoting safety and efficiency on our roads. For instance, AI can alert drivers to unexpected hazards or delays, reducing frustration and enhancing travel safety. Furthermore, the integration of this data with navigation systems means that directions are constantly optimized to inform drivers of the quickest and safest routes available (Petrenko, 2025).

Predictive Analysis

Predictive analysis using AI plays an integral role in forecasting traffic patterns. By examining historical data alongside real-time inputs, AI systems can accurately predict when traffic might be heavier or lighter on specific routes. This feature makes it possible to plan your commute knowing exactly when congestion will occur and which roads to avoid. Such foresight enables travelers to select optimal travel times and manage their daily schedules more effectively. Predictive analytics doesn't just benefit individual commuters; city planners and traffic managers use it to anticipate peak periods and devise strategies for easing congestion, making cities more livable and sustainable (Verma, 2024).

Route Optimization Algorithms

Another essential facet of AI in travel is route optimization algorithms. These smart algorithms work out the most efficient paths by considering multiple factors like distance, speed limits, and real-time road conditions. It's like having a personal assistant continuously adjusting your journey for maximum efficiency. With route optimization, fuel consumption can be minimized, saving costs for users and reducing pollution. This method supports environmental sustainability by actively contributing to lower carbon emissions through smarter driving decisions.

Shared Mobility Solutions

The strength of AI lies not only in helping individual drivers but also in promoting wider societal benefits. AI's capability to facilitate shared mobility solutions is particularly noteworthy. By coordinating services such as carpooling, ride-sharing, and bike-sharing, AI reduces the number of vehicles on the road. This diminishes urban congestion and decreases air pollution levels, contributing to cleaner and more eco-friendly cities. AI algorithms match passengers with similar destinations efficiently, optimizing vehicle occupancy and ensuring the smooth operation of these shared services without unnecessary waiting times (Petrenko, 2025).

AI's impact on traffic management extends into shared transportation infrastructure. For instance, adaptive traffic signals managed by AI adjust timings based on current flow, minimizing idle time for vehicles and pedestrians alike. These intelligent systems respond dynamically to changing conditions, improving traffic throughput and making commutes faster and more reliable. Real-world applications, like those implemented in Pittsburgh when the city introduced Move PGH in 2022, a scheme to make shared mobility options more accessible and car ownership obsolete, showcase dramatic improvements in travel time and reductions in vehicle emissions, demonstrating the tangible benefits of AI-driven traffic solutions (Herbert, 2022)

Guidelines

Alongside these technological advancements, implementing guidelines can significantly enhance the usability and effectiveness of AI in navigation and traffic management.

- Real-time traffic monitoring should be prioritized for both private and public sectors. Authorities can invest in deploying comprehensive sensors and GPS systems to collect data seamlessly across the network.

- By adopting predictive traffic analysis, transportation departments can develop advanced models that forecast traffic patterns with high accuracy. Collaborations with technology firms can help refine these predictions, ensuring they are actionable and relevant.

- Route optimization features should be integrated into all modern navigation systems. These systems could offer options that prioritize eco-friendly routes, even for short trips around the city, encouraging greener commuting habits among users.

- Shared mobility solutions need streamlined platforms for user interaction. User-friendly apps must be developed to make these services accessible and popular, fostering a culture of cooperative commuting.

AI in Public Transport Scheduling

Improving the efficiency and usability of public transportation through AI is transforming how we move within urban environments. The advent of AI technologies promises a future where transit systems are more responsive, accessible, and efficient, contributing to an enhanced commuting experience for everyone involved.

Dynamic Scheduling

Dynamic scheduling powered by AI is a pivotal advancement, addressing one of the most common complaints of public transportation users: inflexible schedules. Traditionally, timetables are set in stone, failing to accommodate fluctuations in demand throughout the day or week. With AI, these outdated methods are being replaced by dynamic algorithms that adjust schedules in real-time based on current and predicted user demand. This means buses and trains can run more frequently during peak hours and scale back during off-peak times, optimizing resource allocation and reducing unnecessary fuel usage (Terekhov, 2024).

A practical guideline for implementing dynamic scheduling involves integrating AI algorithms with existing transport infrastructure to monitor passenger flow. This allows transit authorities to make data-driven decisions that improve punctuality and overall service quality. For instance, AI-powered systems could suggest adding extra vehicles during events or adverse weather conditions, ensuring that supply meets demand without over-committing resources.

Intuitive, User-Friendly Applications

AI enhances the usability of public transport through intuitive, user-friendly applications that deliver timely updates and information. Commuters no longer need to rely on static timetables or guesswork to plan their journeys. Modern apps, equipped with AI capabilities, provide real-time notifications about delays, route changes, and vehicle availability. Such interfaces not only offer convenience but also empower commuters by enabling them to make informed travel choices, potentially diverting to alternative routes if disruptions occur.

Demand-Response AI Solutions

Demand-responsive AI solutions offer another significant benefit by tailoring services to specific community needs. Unlike traditional fixed-route models, demand-responsive systems allow for flexibility in routes and timings, effectively serving less-populated or remote areas that usually suffer from insufficient transport options. By analyzing various data points—including geographical, demographic, and historical travel patterns—AI systems can deploy resources where they are most needed. For example, smaller shuttle services can be automatically dispatched to areas experiencing sudden spikes in demand, ensuring that all regions receive equitable access to public transportation services (Iyer, 2021).

Improvements in Infrastructure

AI's role in enhancing public transport extends to infrastructure improvements. By analyzing vast amounts of data collected from sensors and Internet of Things (IoT) devices, AI helps identify patterns and pinpoint areas requiring investment or upgrades. This analysis guides smart infrastructure investments that not only support current operational demands but are also future-proofed against emerging trends and challenges. For instance, AI might reveal the need for additional bike racks near train stations or highlight the potential benefits of dedicated bus lanes in high-traffic areas.

These enhancements contribute to environmental sustainability. With AI optimizing routes and schedules, public transport systems can reduce their carbon footprint significantly. Efficient use of resources leads to lower fuel consumption and decreased emissions, supporting broader efforts to combat climate change while still meeting the mobility needs of growing urban populations.

In major cities around the globe, AI-driven traffic management systems have successfully eased congestion and improved travel speeds. Cities embracing these technologies report increased passenger satisfaction, more consistent ride experiences, and noticeable reductions in operational costs (Vujadinovic et al., 2024). AI thus paves the way for an even smarter, interconnected future in urban transportation.

Travel Safety and Security Enhancements

In today's ever-evolving world of travel, ensuring safety and security has emerged as a priority for many travelers. AI technologies have stepped in to address these concerns, offering unprecedented solutions that not only promise peace of mind but also act proactively against potential threats. Let's delve into how these innovations are reshaping our travel experiences.

AI-Backed Monitoring Systems

AI-backed monitoring systems have increased safety across travel hubs such as airports and train stations. These systems are equipped with advanced surveillance capabilities that can detect suspicious behaviors in real-time. By analyzing patterns through machine learning, AI helps identify potential threats before they become a problem, thereby deterring criminal activities before they escalate. For instance, cameras with facial recognition software can alert security personnel if known offenders or individuals with flagged profiles are detected within secure areas, significantly enhancing public safety.

Fraud Detection

When it comes to financial transactions in travel, AI's fraud detection capabilities are invaluable. Travel bookings often involve large sums of money, making them an attractive target for cybercriminals. Incorporating AI-driven fraud detection mechanisms helps protect travelers by scrutinizing every transaction for anomalies. Machine learning algorithms analyze vast amounts of payment data to recognize patterns typical of fraudulent activities. This proactive approach ensures that unauthorized access or potentially harmful transactions are swiftly flagged and addressed, keeping travelers' finances secure and mitigating risks associated with credit card fraud or identity theft.

Emergency Response Systems

Another crucial development is in emergency response systems utilizing AI technology. In situations requiring rapid crisis management, time is of the essence. AI systems can quickly assess the nature and scale of an emergency by synthesizing information from various data points—like local sensor feeds and communication networks—to coordinate an effective response. For example, if a natural disaster strikes while someone is traveling, AI can assist in predicting its impact, allowing airlines to reroute flights or advising tourists on safe evacuation routes. Such capabilities greatly enhance the effectiveness of emergency preparedness, ensuring that help is deployed efficiently and accurately.

Personal Safety Apps

AI-powered personal safety apps have gained popularity among travelers seeking additional resources and guidance for safe travels. These applications offer features such as real-time location sharing, virtual escort services, and SOS functionalities that can be activated instantly in case of distress. They provide users with immediate access to emergency contacts, local authorities, and even medical assistance, should the need arise. As an added benefit, these apps often include practical advice tailored to specific destinations, offering insights on areas to avoid and tips for maintaining personal safety throughout one's journey (Giordano, 2024).

Guidelines

It's essential to remember some guidelines when using personal safety devices and apps.

- Testing the functionality of new equipment before reliance is critical, ensuring familiarity with features like alarms or SOS triggers (Giordano, 2024).

- Creating a plan involving emergency contacts prepares both the traveler and their network for swift action in crisis scenarios, reinforcing the overall sense of security.

Final Insights

AI is revolutionizing travel planning and transport by offering a suite of tools that cater to the diverse needs of modern travelers. From crafting personalized itineraries based on your unique interests to dynamically adjusting plans in real-time, AI takes the stress out of trip preparation. It ensures your journey is tailored just for you, whether you're seeking adventure, relaxation, or a mix of both. Additionally, collaborative planning features allow groups to effortlessly sync individual preferences, ensuring a harmonious and enjoyable travel experience for everyone involved.

Moving toward the future, utilizing these AI-driven technologies will not only simplify our travels but also empower us with smarter decision-making. By embracing AI's budget-friendly recommendations, adaptable itineraries, and group-planning capabilities, travelers can enjoy seamless adventures without unnecessary hassles. Whether you're a tech enthusiast curious about AI's capabilities or a busy professional wanting efficient trip management, these innovations promise to enhance every aspect of your travel, making it more personalized, cost-effective, and enjoyable than ever before.

Chapter 8:

Overcoming AI Adoption

Challenges

While the possibilities of AI are endless, it's common for misconceptions and fears to cloud its adoption. Many find themselves asking if AI will invade their privacy or even replace human roles. These uncertainties can create barriers that prevent people from fully embracing the benefits AI offers. By tackling these concerns head-on, we can demystify AI and help users see how it can complement rather than complicate our lives. Through addressing these fears, AI can transform from an elusive concept into a practical tool for personal and professional growth.

This chapter provides a roadmap for overcoming AI adoption challenges by focusing on several key areas. We'll delve into security aspects, discussing how data protection measures like encryption lay the groundwork for safe and secure AI use. We also consider how to empower individuals to manage their personal data preferences and underscore the importance of transparency in AI processes.

By shedding light on how AI makes decisions, you will gain insights into making informed choices about AI integration. Additionally, we'll discuss real-world applications that showcase AI's role in enhancing job functions and productivity. Understanding these facets will not only address common myths but also equip you with the confidence needed to incorporate AI into your daily routines effectively.

Understanding AI Security and Privacy Concerns

In the rapidly advancing technological landscape, AI stands out as a compelling force. Yet, as enthusiastic as many are about its potential, fears about data security and privacy can create significant hesitations. Understanding how to address these concerns is key to fostering confidence in AI adoption, particularly concerning sensitive information.

Data Encryption

A cornerstone in securing user trust is data encryption. This method is vital for safeguarding sensitive information from unauthorized access. Encryption acts like a digital lock, turning readable data into an encoded format that only authorized parties can decode with the correct key. Such protection is necessary as cyber threats continue to evolve, making it imperative for organizations and individuals to prioritize secure communication channels and databases. Many users might not realize it, but every time they send an email or make a transaction online, encryption plays a role in protecting their information. Thus, increasing awareness of encryption technology not only mitigates risk but also enhances user confidence. According to Skyflow, a leading company in data protection, implementing robust encryption standards is crucial for maintaining compliance with regulations while ensuring data remains secure (Ovick & Wu, 2024).

Empowering Users

Empowering users with control over their personal data-sharing preferences is crucial in reducing anxiety about privacy. When individuals have the power to decide what data they share and with whom, their comfort level with AI systems significantly increases. This autonomy encourages trust and ensures that users remain in control of their digital footprint. Organizations that prioritize user-driven data governance often see higher levels of engagement and satisfaction.

Therefore, it's essential for entities deploying AI solutions to implement clear interfaces that allow users to manage their data preferences easily. Explicit consent before data collection exemplifies this approach, emphasizing transparency and respect for user autonomy.

Additionally, explaining how user data will be utilized in non-technical language can enhance understanding and trust. Encouragingly, guidelines are emerging to aid organizations in establishing effective user control mechanisms. These guidelines recommend designing intuitive settings that permit easy adjustments to data-sharing preferences, thus placing the user firmly in charge (Wilhelm, 2024).

Transparency in AI

The mystique surrounding AI's operational mechanics can also contribute to apprehension. Transparency in AI systems helps demystify these processes, providing users with a window into how decisions are made. Essentially, transparency involves openly communicating about the AI's function, the data it uses, and its decision-making criteria.

This openness helps dispel myths about AI being an opaque "black box" and allows users to comprehend its underlying logic. For instance, when using AI for recommendations in retail or healthcare, elucidating why certain suggestions are made based on collected data can increase user acceptance and trust.

By doing so, users feel more secure and engaged with the technology they depend on daily. Moreover, adopting a clear and straightforward communication style in AI explanations makes technical information accessible to all audience members, regardless of their background. This commitment to transparency aligns with growing demands for accountable and ethical AI practices.

Regulations

The existence of regulations governing AI use plays a vital role in protecting consumers and acting as safeguards against misuse. Regulations such as The General Data Protection Regulation (GDPR) in Europe and similar laws worldwide set stringent rules on data handling and privacy, forcing companies to adhere to high standards of data protection. These frameworks ensure that organizations are accountable for mishandling data and encourage responsible development and deployment of AI technologies.

Compliance with these regulations extends beyond legal obligation—it represents a commitment to ethical AI use. Companies integrating AI must view this compliance not as a hurdle but as a strategic opportunity to build trust and showcase their dedication to user protection. Skyflow exemplifies this by embedding zero-trust security models in its operations to meet complex regulatory demands while prioritizing innovation (Ovick & Wu, 2024). Guidelines suggest businesses should regularly audit their systems to ensure continuous alignment with evolving regulations and actualize privacy-centric business strategies.

Debunking AI Myths

It's not uncommon for individuals to harbor reservations rooted in myths and misconceptions surrounding AI. Some common myths about AI include:

- **AI Can Think Like Humans:** Many believe that AI possesses human-like thought processes and emotions, but it operates based on algorithms and data, lacking true understanding.

- **AI Will Replace Humans:** There's a fear that AI will completely replace human jobs, but it's more likely that AI will augment human capabilities and create new job opportunities.

- **AI is Infallible:** People often think AI is perfect and makes no mistakes. In reality, AI can have biases and errors based on the data it has been trained on.

- **AI Understands Context:** While AI can analyze data and recognize patterns, it doesn't fully comprehend context like humans do.

- **AI is Sentient:** Some believe AI has consciousness or self-awareness, but it operates purely on programming and data processing without any sense of self.

- **AI Can Operate Independently:** Many think AI can function autonomously without human intervention. While some systems can automate processes, they still require human oversight and guidance.

- **All AI Tools Are the Same:** There's a misconception that all AI works in the same way. There are various types of AI with different capabilities and applications.

These myths can lead to misunderstandings about what AI is and how it can be used effectively. We will look at two common myths about AI in depth below.

AI Is Stealing Our Jobs

One such common belief is the fear that AI will diminish human roles by automating tasks traditionally handled by people. However, this concern overlooks the potential of AI to enhance job functions rather than eliminate them. AI often serves as a tool to streamline repetitive processes, which allows professionals to engage in more strategic and creative endeavors. For instance, automation of data entry empowers employees to focus on analysis and strategy. This shift not only preserves jobs but also creates new ones tailored to managing and interpreting AI-driven insights.

Take recruitment as an example; AI can conduct initial resume screenings, freeing up human recruiters to concentrate on building relationships with potential candidates—a task far more intricate and nuanced than mere screening. Hence, the introduction of AI into a professional setting typically augments human capability, fostering innovation and facilitating the emergence of new job sectors that require both technical and creative skills (AI in Hiring: 7 Myths You Need to Stop Believing, n.d.).

AI systems excel at processing large datasets at high speed, identifying trends, and suggesting patterns that might escape human notice. Still, they are fundamentally reliant on the quality and structure of the data they process. Human insight remains crucial, especially when it comes to making decisions that require contextual understanding and ethical judgment—areas where AI's current capabilities don't suffice. For example, AI might analyze sales data and predict customer behavior but cannot replace the strategic expertise required to craft and implement effective marketing campaigns. Thus, AI acts as a supportive tool that enhances decision-making rather than making choices autonomously (Lim, 2025).

AI Is Exclusively Used by Tech-Savvy People

Another misunderstanding is that AI is exclusive to tech-savvy individuals, limiting its utility to those with advanced computer science degrees. However, in reality, modern user-friendly AI tools are becoming increasingly accessible to people across various disciplines, even those without a technical background. These tools are designed with intuitive interfaces, requiring minimal training to operate effectively.

For curious individuals, platforms that feature drag-and-drop functionalities or pre-built templates provide an easy entry point to experiment with AI technologies like predictive analytics or machine learning models. By lowering the barrier to entry, these tools encourage widespread exploration and integration of AI into daily tasks, making it possible for virtually anyone to harness the benefits of AI without having to decode complex programming languages.

Building Tech-Savvy Mindsets

Developing a mindset that embraces technology, particularly AI, is critical in everyday life as the world becomes increasingly digital. Developing a mindset conducive to embracing AI revolves around being proactive, curious, and willing to engage in continuous learning and experimentation. Each of the points below—lifelong learning, experimentation, solution orientation, and community engagement—plays a vital role in demystifying AI and integrating it seamlessly into our lives. This holistic approach not only alleviates fears and misconceptions about AI but also empowers individuals to harness its full potential for personal and societal advancement.

Value Lifelong Learning

The first step toward cultivating a tech-savvy mindset is acknowledging the importance of lifelong learning. Adaptability is key to staying relevant and effective. Lifelong learning encourages individuals to be open to new information and skills. By embracing lifelong learning, we enhance our personal growth and position ourselves to take advantage of emerging opportunities in technology.

To cultivate lifelong learning, set personal learning goals and seek resources that align with these objectives. Whether through online courses, workshops, or simply reading about the latest developments in AI, staying informed ensures we remain adaptable to changes around us. Engaging with this practice helps demystify AI, making it less intimidating and more approachable for everyday use (Zawacki-Richter et al., 2019).

Embrace Experimentation

An experimental attitude towards AI encourages discovery through trial and error. Much like scientists conducting experiments, being open to trying new tools and technologies can lead to unexpected insights and breakthroughs. This does not mean every experiment will yield success; rather, each attempt is an opportunity to learn, adjust, and improve. For instance, experimenting with AI-driven productivity apps can reveal which tools best suit your workflow, ultimately enhancing efficiency and effectiveness.

To cultivate an experimental attitude, start by identifying simple tasks in your daily routine where AI could assist. Implement small trials using AI applications designed for those tasks. Evaluate the outcomes critically, noting what worked well and what didn't, and be prepared to make adjustments along the way. Over time, these small experiments build confidence and familiarity with AI technologies, reducing the anxiety often associated with adopting new systems (Walter, 2024).

Be Solution-Oriented

Adopting a solution-oriented approach motivates us to leverage AI for addressing real-world challenges. AI's potential to transform industries and solve complex problems is immense, from optimizing supply chains to enhancing medical diagnostics. By focusing on how AI can offer tangible solutions, we shift from viewing it as a threat to seeing it as a valuable tool for improvement.

To effectively use AI in problem-solving, it is vital to clearly define the issues you wish to address and identify how AI can be applied. Consider analyzing data trends through AI models to uncover patterns that aid decision-making or automate repetitive tasks that free up time for strategic thinking. This approach aligns with the broader goals of boosting productivity and achieving greater efficiency in both personal and professional settings (Chiu et al., 2023).

Engage With Technology Communities

Engaging with technology communities can significantly broaden your understanding of AI while providing peer support. Technology communities create platforms for sharing knowledge, experiences, and challenges, nurturing a collaborative learning environment.

Participating in forums, online groups, or local meetups dedicated to AI can expose individuals to diverse perspectives and innovative ideas.

Engage with these communities by sharing your experiences, asking questions, and offering assistance where possible. This reciprocal exchange builds networks that can provide support, inspiration, and motivation. Networking with others who share similar interests or have more experience in AI can expand your capabilities and offer insights into overcoming common hurdles, further embedding AI into daily life.

Navigating AI Ethics and Biases

Addressing ethical concerns and biases in AI usage is pivotal to fostering responsible interactions with technology. As AI becomes increasingly embedded in our daily lives, understanding the ethical frameworks surrounding its design and development promotes a deeper awareness of responsible practices.

Ownership Rights and Infringements

One critical aspect of ethical AI involves defining clear guidelines regarding ownership rights and potential infringements. This understanding not only shapes equitable digital spaces but also facilitates more transparent engagements between creators and AI developers (The Ethical Considerations of Artificial Intelligence 2023). Here are some examples of ownership rights and infringements associated with AI:

- **Copyright Ownership:** If an AI program creates original artwork, music, or literature, the question arises as to who owns the copyright— the developer of the AI, the user who prompted it, or the AI itself.

- **Patent Rights:** Inventions produced by AI can lead to disputes over patent ownership. If an AI invents a new product, it can be unclear whether the inventor is the AI, its programmer, or the entity that owns the AI.

- **Data Ownership:** AI systems require data to function effectively. Issues can arise over who owns the data used to train AI, especially when it includes personal or sensitive information.

- **Licensing Agreements:** The use of AI tools often comes with licensing agreements that specify how the AI can be used and any restrictions. Violating these terms may result in infringements.

- **Trademark Infringement:** AI-generated content that resembles existing trademarks can lead to claims of trademark infringement, especially if it causes confusion among consumers.

- **Plagiarism:** AI-generated works that closely mimic existing works can lead to accusations of plagiarism, raising questions of originality and ownership.

- **Fair Use:** The use of AI-generated content may raise fair use concerns, particularly when the content is based on copyrighted material.

These issues highlight the complexities of ownership and rights in the context of AI and the need for clear legal frameworks.

Identifying and Mitigating Biases in AI Applications

Identifying and mitigating biases within AI applications are at the forefront of responsible AI use. AI systems often inherit biases from their training data, which can lead to discriminatory outcomes. For instance, AI-driven recruitment tools may unwittingly perpetuate gender or racial biases if trained on historically skewed data sets. To combat this, regular ethical risk assessments are vital. These assessments help identify potential risks before deploying AI systems and ensure they align with fairness and accountability principles (Lumenalta, 2024). By prioritizing vigilance in evaluation, organizations can actively work to prevent biased outputs and promote more equitable solutions.

Inclusive AI practices emerge from assembling diverse teams that reflect a wide range of perspectives. Diverse development teams are crucial in creating AI solutions that cater to various cultures, needs, and preferences. This inclusivity uplifts underrepresented voices and ensures that AI technologies achieve better outcomes for all users.

For example, engaging stakeholders from varied backgrounds play a significant role in refining product recommendations in sectors such as e-commerce, ensuring that diversity is mirrored in customer experiences (Lumenalta, 2024). Empowering diverse teams facilitates advocacy efforts and strengthens the development and implementation of inclusive AI tools.

Personal Responsibility

Personal responsibility in interacting with AI is another fundamental ethical consideration. Individuals interacting with AI bear a certain level of personal responsibility that mirrors broader societal implications. Educating users about ethical AI principles, transparency, and the limitations of AI systems is crucial. Users need to remain mindful of how AI decisions may affect them personally and societally, encouraging a culture of critical engagement and vigilant adoption.

For example, empowering healthcare professionals with AI literacy builds trust in AI-driven insights and helps improve patient outcomes (Lumenalta, 2024). When individuals engage with AI responsibly, it fosters an environment where technology enhances human capabilities rather than detracts from them.

Guidelines

Guidelines for identifying biases and promoting inclusive practices are essential for ethical AI implementation.

- Biases should be systematically evaluated by applying fairness measures and ensuring ongoing monitoring of AI systems.

- Regular ethical risk assessments help pinpoint areas susceptible to bias, allowing organizations to address them proactively.

- Diverse development teams are encouraged to collaborate on projects, bringing multiple perspectives to tackle biases and promote inclusivity effectively.

- Creating channels for user feedback further refines AI systems, encouraging ongoing improvement while ensuring alignment with ethical standards (Lumenalta, 2024).

Final Insights

We've explored the essential elements of understanding AI security and debunked common myths that cloud its potential. We've explored the complexities of data encryption and user privacy preferences, emphasizing how these measures not only safeguard information but also build trust in AI systems. By giving users control over their data and adopting transparent AI practices, we can alleviate fears surrounding AI as a mysterious "black box." Dispelling worries about job displacement, we highlighted how AI complements human roles by enhancing productivity rather than replacing it. By promoting a collaborative dialog on AI's limitations and capabilities, we pave the way for more confident and informed adoption.

Furthermore, the discussion underscored important aspects like regulations and ethical considerations that guide responsible AI usage. The existence of global compliance frameworks serves as a pillar for protecting consumer interests while maintaining high standards of data protection. We also addressed the accessibility of AI tools, making it evident that they are not just reserved for the tech elite.

Whether you're a curious adult, a busy professional, or someone focused on personal growth, engaging in continuous learning and experimentation empowers you to harness AI effectively. As we navigate these considerations, the key takeaway remains clear: awareness, transparency, and education are vital in ensuring that AI technology becomes a practical and trusted ally in our day-to-day lives.

Chapter 9:

Cultivating a Tech-Embracing

Mindset

Cultivating a tech-embracing mindset is about opening our eyes to the vast opportunities that AI and digital tools offer today. In an era where technology is rapidly evolving, it's easy to feel left behind or overwhelmed by new terms and concepts. Yet, embracing these advancements can transform our lives for the better. By shifting how we perceive these innovations, we enable ourselves to harness AI for our growth, tapping into its potential to improve everyday life. Engaging with technology doesn't mean surrendering to it but rather using it as a stepping stone to achieving more than we might have thought possible.

Throughout this chapter, we'll explore the essentials of developing a tech-embracing mindset, including a breakdown of fundamental AI concepts that may initially seem intimidating. Instead of shying away, we'll try and demystify these terms and explore practical ways to integrate them into your daily routine. We'll also discuss how consistently honing our skills through reliable digital resources can place us ahead of the curve, ensuring we're not only keeping pace with but actively shaping the technological environment around us. This chapter aims to equip you with the knowledge and confidence to embrace technology meaningfully.

Developing Digital Literacy

Cultivating a tech-embracing mindset is vital for anyone looking to thrive in a world increasingly dominated by artificial intelligence and digital tools. This section aims to demystify AI fundamentals and provide pragmatic guidance on how individuals can integrate these technologies to enhance their personal and professional lives.

Understand the Basics

To begin with, understanding the basics of AI is crucial. Artificial intelligence refers to systems designed to mimic human intelligence, capturing insights from vast data sets to perform tasks that usually require cognitive functions like learning, reasoning, or problem-solving. Familiarizing yourself with common AI terminologies, such as machine learning, neural networks, and natural language processing, helps bridge the gap between abstract technology concepts and their real-world applications.

- **Natural language processing (NLP)** involves the ability of a computer program to understand, interpret, and manipulate human language in a valuable way. NLP combines computational linguistics—rule-based modeling of human language—with machine learning and deep learning models. The ultimate goal of NLP is to enable computers to comprehend and generate human language in a manner that is both meaningful and useful.

- **Neural networks** consist of interconnected groups of artificial neurons that work together to process information. They can learn from data, recognize patterns, and make decisions.

- **Machine learning** refers to algorithms that allow computers to learn from data patterns without explicit programming.

Understanding these terms will enrich your vocabulary and equip you with the necessary knowledge to discern various AI-driven services and tools.

Explore Digital Resources

Exploring reliable digital resources paves the way for learning more about AI and its practical applications. From online courses on platforms like Coursera and Khan Academy to informative articles on sites like Medium, the internet offers a treasure trove of educational materials accessible at your fingertips. Engaging with communities on forums such as Reddit and Stack Exchange also provides opportunities to connect with experts and peers who share common interests and goals. By leveraging these resources, individuals can stay abreast of technological advancements and continuously hone their skills, ultimately positioning themselves to make the most out of emerging technologies.

Navigating the digital resource landscape can be overwhelming, which is why it's important to identify trustworthy sources. Prioritize resources affiliated with reputable organizations or institutions known for their expertise in tech education. These include academic institutions, established tech companies, and respected publications that often offer certification programs or free courses aimed at educating individuals about foundational and advanced AI topics.

Develop Critical Evaluation Skills

Developing critical evaluation skills is vital when assessing tech solutions. Not all digital tools are created equal; some may claim to offer groundbreaking capabilities yet fall short upon closer inspection. To navigate this terrain effectively, you should consider factors such as ease of use, compatibility with existing systems, and cost-effectiveness. Conducting thorough research, reading user reviews, and even taking advantage of trial periods or demos can significantly aid in making informed decisions. As AI systems become more integral to daily life, it is essential to understand how they impact society and individual rights, ensuring that these tools do not perpetuate biases or compromise personal data integrity (Baig & Khan, 2024).

Adopt Safe Online Practices

A critical aspect of embracing tech responsibly is safe online practices. With cyber threats becoming more sophisticated, maintaining privacy and security online is of utmost importance. Adopting strong password habits, enabling two-factor authentication, and staying vigilant against phishing attempts can protect sensitive information from cybercriminals. It is equally important to update software regularly to patch vulnerabilities and consider using security-focused browsers and virtual private networks (VPNs) to shield online activities. Teaching children about internet safety, as AI does through platforms like Interland, fosters a culture of security awareness from an early age (Sahota, 2024).

Guidelines for building a safe digital environment include practicing proactive measures that safeguard individuals and encourage responsible behavior online. These practices should be seamlessly integrated into everyday routines to enhance digital security. Regularly reviewing security settings across devices can ensure that they align with current privacy needs and vulnerabilities. Additionally, educating oneself and others about evolving cyber threats and responses bolsters defense mechanisms and promotes collective digital safety.

Embracing Change and Innovation

Embracing technological change is essential for personal and professional growth. The rapidly evolving landscape of AI and other emerging technologies can seem daunting at first; however, adopting a positive attitude toward these changes opens up exciting opportunities for advancement and personal development.

Recognize the Advantages

Recognizing the advantages of adapting to new technologies is crucial. Technological advancements offer unique chances to enhance efficiency, improve productivity, and create innovative solutions to everyday challenges. For busy professionals seeking to streamline their work processes, AI tools can automate repetitive tasks, allowing more time to focus on higher-level strategic planning and decision-making.

By actively looking for ways technology can assist in routine operations, individuals can unlock new levels of productivity and drive career progression. Moreover, engaging with technology often encourages creativity and problem-solving skills, as it encourages exploring novel approaches and solutions that might have otherwise gone unnoticed.

Overcome Fears and Anxieties About New Technologies

Embracing technological change isn't without its challenges. One of the most significant barriers is resistance due to fear or uncertainty about new systems. Many people are apprehensive about learning about new tools, fearing they might fail or be replaced by machines. To overcome these fears, it's important to understand their roots and tackle them head-on. Often, this resistance stems from concerns about job security, privacy, or simply the discomfort of stepping out of your comfort zone.

Understanding these root causes is the first step toward addressing them effectively. Communication is crucial here; providing clear information about how technology will benefit both individuals and organizations can alleviate fears. Regular training sessions and workshops can equip individuals with the skills they need to use new tools with confidence, while also highlighting real-life success stories of technological adaptation.

Engage With Innovators and Early Adaptors

Engaging with innovators and early adopters can provide valuable insights and encouragement for those hesitant about change. By connecting with technology enthusiasts, individuals can learn about the practical applications and potential benefits of various tools firsthand. Networking with people who have successfully integrated new technologies into their workflows offers a chance to share experiences and gather tips on best practices.

This engagement nurtures a sense of community around innovation, making the process less intimidating and more collaborative. For example, attending technology-focused meetups or forums can introduce individuals to industry leaders who have navigated similar paths, providing inspiration and motivation to experiment with new tools themselves.

Develop a Growth Mindset

Cultivating a growth mindset, where continuous learning and openness to trying new things are valued, is another critical element in promoting adaptability. As Carol Dweck elaborates in her research on mindsets, embracing a growth mindset involves viewing challenges as opportunities to develop skills rather than as threats (Dweck, 2016). Those who approach technology with curiosity and a willingness to learn tend to adapt more easily. They see each new technological development as a chance to expand their capabilities and keep their skill sets relevant in a rapidly changing environment.

Encouraging an organizational culture that rewards experimentation and values learning from failures can significantly contribute to building this mindset. Celebrating small wins and acknowledging efforts made towards integration can go a long way in maintaining enthusiasm and momentum.

Guidelines

Guidelines to foster this growth-oriented approach include:

- Setting realistic goals for technology usage and regularly assessing progress. Start with small, achievable targets such as integrating one new tool at a time or dedicating a specific amount of time per week to learning its features. Gradually expanding these efforts ensures steady progress without overwhelming individuals or teams.

- Create a supportive environment where questions are encouraged and assistance is readily available. This helps maintain a positive attitude toward ongoing learning. Implementing mentorship programs where seasoned users guide newcomers can also ease transitions and build confidence in using new technologies.

- To ensure that technological adoption translates into tangible growth, measure outcomes and adjust strategies as necessary. Regularly evaluating the impact of new tools on productivity or quality of life helps refine approaches and set future directions. Feedback mechanisms such as surveys or informal check-ins allow individuals to voice their concerns and suggestions, ensuring continuous improvement and alignment with organizational goals.

Setting Realistic AI Expectations

Adapting to AI requires a clear understanding of its strengths and weaknesses. For those intrigued by AI's prospects but daunted by its complexity, embracing a balanced mindset is key. By setting realistic expectations and understanding the interplay between technology and human judgment, AI can become an invaluable ally in both personal and professional realms. It's about finding the right mix—using AI to amplify what humans do best while maintaining control over decisions that demand a human touch. We look at how you can set realistic expectations around AI below.

Appreciate AI's Limitations

It's crucial to grasp the limitations of AI to separate realistic expectations from common misconceptions. Artificial intelligence is undeniably powerful in processing vast amounts of data and recognizing patterns. However, it doesn't possess human qualities like emotion or ethical judgment. It's essential to recognize that AI acts as a tool rather than a replacement for human insight. This nuanced understanding allows you to use AI to its fullest potential without falling into the trap of believing it's infallible.

Set Achievable Goals

As we dive deeper into AI's role in personal and professional settings, setting achievable goals is paramount. For instance, if you're looking to enhance productivity at work by incorporating AI tools, it helps to identify specific tasks where AI can assist while remaining aware of its limitations. A practical approach might be automating routine administrative tasks such as scheduling or data entry, which frees you up for more strategic endeavors. If you are using AI for personal development, AI can offer personalized insights, like tracking fitness goals or suggesting learning paths based on your interests. However, remember that these tools should guide rather than dictate your journey. Establishing clear objectives ensures that AI fits seamlessly into your lifestyle and career ambitions without overwhelming you.

Consider AI's Real World Applications

To further illustrate AI's potential, let's explore its real-world applications and their impact on productivity. One compelling example comes from the healthcare industry, where AI algorithms support doctors by analyzing medical images to detect early signs of diseases like cancer. By doing so, AI enhances diagnostic accuracy while allowing physicians to focus on patient care. Another example involves the finance sector, where AI-driven predictive analytics help businesses anticipate market trends and make informed decisions. These examples highlight how AI, when thoughtfully integrated, can drive efficiency and innovation across diverse fields.

Balance AI's Capabilities With Human Judgment

Balancing AI's capabilities with human judgment remains critical. Human intuition and experience provide context and depth that AI lacks. Consider situations that require empathy, creativity, or ethical considerations—areas where human input is irreplaceable. For instance, while an AI tool could suggest the best candidates for a job based on predefined criteria, human insight is necessary to evaluate cultural fit and potential for growth within a team. Emphasizing the synergy between AI and human decision-making enhances outcomes by leveraging the strengths of both.

Guidelines

Consider creating a structured plan to integrate AI into your daily life effectively. Begin by identifying areas where AI can add value, whether it's automating repetitive tasks, enhancing decision-making, or providing personalized insights. Then set clear, attainable goals tailored to your needs and lifestyle. Remember to continuously evaluate how well these AI tools serve their purpose and adjust your strategies accordingly.

Incorporating AI doesn't mean surrendering control; instead, it's about harnessing technology to complement and augment human abilities. This partnership can foster creativity and innovation, encouraging new ways of thinking and doing.

Aligning AI Use With Personal Values

Developing a tech-embracing mindset is not just about adapting to new tools but aligning your AI usage with personal beliefs and values. This alignment encourages authenticity and ensures that technology serves your needs rather than the other way around.

Identify Your Personal Values

To begin this alignment process, it's essential to identify your personal values. These values act as a compass, guiding you in selecting technology that resonates with your individual beliefs. For instance, if privacy is a core value, you may prioritize tools that offer robust data protection features. Take time to reflect on what truly matters to you—whether it's environmental sustainability, community engagement, or innovation—and let those principles steer your tech choices.

Choose Ethical AI Tools

Once you've established your values, the next step is choosing ethical AI tools to promote responsible use. Ethical considerations in AI are crucial, especially as concerns about biased algorithms and data misuse grow. Look for AI solutions that champion transparency and fairness and are backed by organizations committed to ethical standards. When these tools align with your values, they not only enhance your life but also build trust in technological practices. According to a report by PwC, 84% of CEOs emphasize the importance of explainable AI decisions for trust building (9 Ethical AI Principles for Organizations to Follow, 2023).

Create a Structured Tech Plan

Creating a structured tech plan is an effective strategy for navigating AI options with intentionality and clarity. Start by mapping out your tech needs and goals, then research tools that fit within this framework.

This plan acts as a roadmap, helping you avoid impulse purchases and focus on acquiring technologies that genuinely support your development. Furthermore, a well-thought-out plan allows you to reevaluate your toolkit periodically, ensuring it remains aligned with evolving preferences and technological advancements.

Evaluate Your Choices

Regular evaluation of how AI aligns with your values is key to consistent personal growth and adaptability. Set aside regular intervals to assess your tech setup. Are the tools still serving their intended purpose? How do they impact your daily routines and overall well-being? Engaging in this reflective practice keeps you attuned to the dynamic nature of both technology and your own priorities. It encourages adaptability, a vital trait in an era of constant change. The Deloitte State of AI 2022 report highlights reliability and robustness as foundational elements of ethical AI, underpinning trust and adaptability (9 Ethical AI Principles for Organizations to Follow, 2023).

Consider, for example, someone who values environmental sustainability. They might opt for AI tools that optimize energy consumption or products manufactured through eco-friendly processes. By constantly checking that their technology stays true to these ideals, they not only capitalize on AI's potential but also contribute positively to their chosen cause. Similarly, a professional concerned about data privacy might regularly audit their AI tools to ensure compliance with the latest security standards and safeguard their information effectively.

Seek Out Like-Minded People

Assembling a team of like-minded individuals can also support your journey in aligning AI tools with personal values. Sharing insights and experiences with others who hold similar beliefs enriches your understanding of available technologies and innovative practices. Collaborative discussions often reveal new approaches or tools you might not have considered independently. This communal approach promotes accountability, offering encouragement and support as you refine your tech plan.

Additionally, leveraging resources such as online forums, webinars, and workshops dedicated to ethical AI can provide valuable guidance. Experts in these fields often share practical tips and case studies that illustrate successful implementations of value-aligned technology. Engaging with this wealth of information empowers you to make informed decisions and stay current with developments in AI ethics.

Final Insights

In this chapter, we've explored the necessity of shifting perspectives to embrace AI as a tool for personal growth. By understanding AI fundamentals and familiarizing ourselves with key terminologies like machine learning and neural networks, we can bridge the gap between abstract concepts and real-world applications. This knowledge empowers us to discern the benefits of various AI-driven tools, enhancing both personal and professional growth. Moreover, utilizing trustworthy digital resources and engaging in continuous learning positions us to navigate emerging technologies successfully. As we face the digital revolution head-on, developing critical evaluation skills ensures we make informed decisions on tech solutions while keeping ethics and privacy at the forefront.

Embracing AI is not only about adapting to technology but also aligning it with our values. By identifying what truly matters, whether it's data privacy or environmental sustainability, we can choose ethical AI tools that resonate with our beliefs. Building a structured plan helps focus on technologies that genuinely support our growth, allowing us to reevaluate and adjust as needed. Collaboration with like-minded individuals and leveraging expert resources further enrich this process, offering diverse insights and encouragement. Ultimately, cultivating a tech-embracing mindset involves an ongoing commitment to introspection and intentional choices, empowering us to leverage AI's transformative capabilities without compromising our principles.

Chapter 10:

Future of AI in Everyday Life

The future of AI is all about how it will integrate into our daily lives, transforming the way we live, work, and grow. One day you will live in a world where your morning starts with an AI assistant that not only brews your coffee but also fine-tunes your day according to weather changes, traffic updates, and critical tasks on your agenda. It's not just science fiction anymore; it's becoming our new reality. As AI continues to evolve, its capabilities expand, offering innovative solutions that enhance productivity and personal development alike. Whether it's optimizing our homes' energy use or providing personalized learning experiences, AI's role in our everyday lives is set to increase over the next few years.

In this chapter, we'll explore the fascinating ways AI is expected to revolutionize our lifestyles. We consider how AI technologies are making life easier through mundane task automation and bringing unprecedented opportunities for creativity and personal growth.

From smart home systems to AI-driven financial management, you'll discover how these advancements promise to provide more than just time-saving benefits. We'll guide you through practical applications and visionary concepts, showcasing how AI is empowering individuals across different walks of life, from busy professionals seeking efficiency to creative minds seeking innovation. By examining these transformative aspects, we equip you with insights on leveraging AI for a more enriched and efficient future.

Predictions for AI Advancements

AI is rapidly embedding itself into everyday life. As AI becomes more ingrained in our lives, its potential to facilitate self-improvement and growth becomes evident. AI-driven platforms personalize learning experiences, adapting lessons to fit individual pace and style, much like having a dedicated tutor available anytime. Such applications are not only convenient but incredibly effective in fostering continuous personal development. They allow learners to access quality education and training across various disciplines without geographical or economic barriers, paving the way for lifelong learning and skill enhancement. We look at how AI is likely to advance in the coming years below.

Increased Access to AI

New AI technologies are advancing and becoming more intuitive and user-friendly, which makes them accessible to a wider audience than ever before. This shift represents a significant leap toward democratizing AI capabilities, allowing individuals from various backgrounds to incorporate these innovations into their daily routines with minimal technical knowledge. For instance, voice-activated virtual assistants like Amazon's Alexa or Apple's Siri can now perform tasks ranging from setting reminders to controlling smart home devices, all through simple voice commands. This level of accessibility opens up a world of possibilities for users who may previously have been intimidated by technology, enabling them to leverage AI for practical, everyday applications.

Improved Productivity

The anticipated breakthroughs in AI are set to revolutionize productivity by providing efficient solutions for routine tasks. Imagine a world where mundane chores are handled effortlessly by AI-powered devices. For example, robot vacuum cleaners equipped with AI can map your home's layout and clean it efficiently while you're at work.

Similarly, AI-driven personal finance apps analyze spending patterns to recommend personalized budgets, helping individuals manage their finances more effectively without manual input. These innovations save time and enhance overall productivity by freeing up mental bandwidth and allowing people to focus on more creative or rewarding pursuits. According to a study, such advancements could potentially give back two weeks per year to the average worker by 2030 (Bieser, 2023).

Empowering Individuals as Creators

Beyond improving productivity, AI tools are increasingly empowering individuals as creators, enabling innovation that surpasses traditional consumer technology use. With AI-generated content, individuals can explore artistic or inventive endeavors that were once limited to those with specialized skills. Programs like OpenAI's DALL-E 2 generate visuals based on textual descriptions, offering artists a new medium to experiment with ideas and concepts.

Similarly, generative design tools used in architecture or industrial design can produce optimized structures and products based on specific criteria, allowing designers to innovate more efficiently. This shift signals a transformative era where anyone can partake in the creative process, blurring the lines between professional creators and hobbyists.

However, it's crucial to acknowledge the balance AI must maintain to avoid stifling creativity. While AI provides novel insights, it also poses a risk of overshadowing the human element essential to innovation. As AI systems become more proficient, they must be designed to augment rather than replace human creativity, maintaining the integrity of uniquely human experiences and interactions that fuel idea generation. The real value lies in a symbiotic relationship where humans guide AI strategically, leveraging its capabilities while staying firmly in control of creative direction.

Encouraging Collaboration

AI's role in promoting creativity does not end at creation but extends to collaboration. AI can identify patterns in large data sets, guiding researchers toward breakthrough hypotheses they might otherwise have overlooked. For instance, machine learning algorithms have been used to predict potential chemical combinations for energy-efficient batteries, highlighting AI's ability to inspire human ingenuity (Bieser, 2023). By collaborating with intelligent systems, individuals and teams can push the boundaries of what's possible, enhancing their creative output significantly.

Impacts of AI on Future Workplaces

AI is set to revolutionize work environments in ways that could redefine how we view our roles and responsibilities. We look at ways in which it is likely to do that below.

Collaboration Between AI and Human Workers

One promising aspect of AI integration lies in its potential for collaboration with human workers, enhancing efficiency, and promoting innovation by complementing human capabilities. Think about the benefits AI provides in sectors like healthcare, where machine learning algorithms assist doctors in diagnosing conditions more swiftly and accurately than ever before. This type of collaboration doesn't replace the doctor but rather amplifies their abilities, leading to better health outcomes. Such applications are expanding across industries, providing an exciting preview of how AI can be a powerful ally in everyday work settings.

Faster Data Processing

In financial services, AI's ability to process vast amounts of data quickly can help human analysts spot trends and risks that might otherwise go unnoticed. The ESCP Business School's research emphasizes how AI adoption accelerates growth within manufacturing, finance, and other sectors. By empowering human workers through enhanced decision-making processes, AI creates opportunities for businesses to innovate and drive economic success (Artificial Intelligence and Productivity: Transforming the Modern Workplace, 2025).

Supporting Flexible Work Structures

Another significant way AI transforms work environments is by supporting flexible work structures. As remote work becomes increasingly viable, AI tools play a crucial role in facilitating effective communication and productivity. For example, virtual assistants powered by AI can provide instant support to remote employees, addressing frequently asked questions and facilitating quick access to information. This reduces time spent on mundane tasks, allowing workers to focus on more strategic initiatives. AI-driven scheduling tools also enable adaptive work arrangements, improving work-life balance by aligning workloads with personal needs and preferences (Singh, 2024).

Real-Time Data Analysis

AI's potential extends into creating real-time data analysis capabilities, which transform the decision-making processes within organizations. By analyzing complex datasets at unprecedented speeds, AI opens new possibilities for businesses to respond to market changes with agility and precision. In dynamic environments where conditions shift rapidly, such as retail or logistics, having AI systems that deliver actionable insights allows companies to remain competitive. AI-driven data analysis helps organizations anticipate consumer behavior and adapt strategies accordingly, guaranteeing resilience amid uncertainty

(Artificial Intelligence and Productivity: Transforming the Modern Workplace, 2025).

A practical example of this in action is seen in supply chain management. AI can predict demand trends, optimize inventory levels, and reduce wastage, all of which contribute to significant cost savings and increased efficiency. As businesses continue to leverage AI's analytical prowess, they position themselves advantageously in the marketplace, reaping both short-term operational gains and long-term innovative achievements.

Thoughtful Implementation

AI integration requires thoughtful implementation to maximize its potential while addressing challenges that might arise. Effective strategies involve aligning AI tools with organizational goals and ensuring ethical considerations remain central throughout the process. Successful AI integration hinges on taking incremental steps, such as conducting pilot projects, to assess performance before full deployment. Organizations must remain vigilant in monitoring AI systems to guarantee transparency and fairness in operations, fostering stakeholder trust.

Such practices highlight the importance of upskilling employees so they can effectively work with AI systems. Training programs that focus on developing digital literacy and familiarity with AI tools ensure that the workforce can optimally harness these technologies, enabling them to thrive in an AI-enhanced environment.

AI in Sustainability and Environmental Conservation

AI not only has the potential to enhance our daily lives but can also play an important role in saving our planet. One of the most exciting prospects of AI lies in its potential to contribute significantly to ecological balance and resource optimization. By leveraging technology, we can move towards a future where natural resources are used efficiently, environmental challenges are tackled with precision, and biodiversity thrives under vigilant stewardship. Let's look at ways we can do just that.

Smart Resource Management

Smart resource management is a prime example of AI's power to transform the way we utilize natural resources. In agriculture, AI-driven systems can predict crop needs more accurately than ever before. By analyzing vast datasets from weather patterns, soil health, and crop varieties, AI can optimize irrigation schedules and fertilizer applications. This reduces waste, as resources are applied only when necessary, thereby supporting sustainable farming practices. Similarly, in industries such as manufacturing, AI can streamline production processes, minimizing excess material use and energy consumption through predictive maintenance and real-time adjustments.

Furthermore, some urban areas have begun integrating AI systems within their infrastructure to create smart cities that manage water, waste, and energy more sustainably. AI optimizes traffic flow, reducing emissions from vehicles idling on congested roads, and adjusts lighting based on human presence to conserve electricity. Through these innovations, AI matches technological growth with environmental stewardship, showcasing that development need not come at the cost of nature.

Environmental Forecasting and Policymaking

The fight against climate change could be bolstered by AI's capabilities, particularly in environmental forecasting and policymaking. AI models can assimilate complex climate data to predict extreme weather events, such as hurricanes or droughts, providing early warnings that allow communities to prepare effectively. Furthermore, AI can assist policymakers by simulating the outcomes of various environmental policies, highlighting the most effective strategies for reducing carbon emissions and enhancing sustainability. These insights offer a scientific basis for crafting policies that ensure long-term environmental health while balancing economic considerations.

Monitoring Ecosystems

When it comes to protecting biodiversity, AI's role becomes even more critical. The capacity of AI to monitor ecosystems in real-time offers unprecedented opportunities for conservation efforts. Drones equipped with AI sensors can survey vast areas of forests or oceans, detecting changes in wildlife populations or signs of illegal activities like poaching and deforestation. Aided by machine learning algorithms, these technologies process immense amounts of data quickly and accurately, alerting conservationists to problems as they arise, rather than after the fact.

A notable illustration of AI's impact can be found in its application to endangered species protection. By utilizing AI-powered image recognition, ecologists can track animal movements and behaviors remotely through camera traps. This data helps understand population dynamics and habitat usage, which are essential for targeted conservation strategies. Such detailed information was previously hard to obtain without intrusive methods that could disturb ecosystems.

Challenges

However, realizing AI's full potential in the field of environmental sustainability requires addressing certain challenges. Access to high-quality, comprehensive datasets remains fundamental to training effective AI models. This necessitates collaboration between governments, industries, and researchers to ensure data sharing while respecting privacy concerns. Moreover, there is a need for increased investments in AI research directed specifically at environmental applications, fostering innovation that directly targets ecological goals.

Another hurdle involves ensuring equitable access to AI technologies globally. While developed nations may lead the charge in AI adoption, developing regions must not be left behind due to technological or financial barriers. This calls for international cooperation and support to distribute AI technologies that can help conserve biodiversity and manage resources across diverse landscapes.

Preparing for AI-driven Future Changes

In the rapidly advancing world of AI, adapting to technological changes is not just a choice but a necessity. AI's potential to revolutionize everyday life is immense, affecting everything from how we work to how we interact with the world around us. To effectively navigate this new landscape, individuals need to be empowered with an understanding of emerging AI technologies. By gaining insight into these technologies, people can make informed decisions and embrace continuous learning, which becomes a cornerstone of personal and professional growth.

Recognize AI's Capabilities and Limitations

Understanding AI begins with recognizing its capabilities and limitations. Emerging AI technologies, such as machine learning algorithms and natural language processing, enable machines to perform tasks that traditionally require human intelligence. These technologies power applications in fields like healthcare, finance, and entertainment, offering tools that are increasingly integrated into our daily lives. For example, AI-driven diagnostic tools in healthcare can analyze medical images more quickly and accurately than human radiologists, while AI in finance automates trading and fraud detection processes. Recognizing how these changes influence various sectors helps individuals appreciate AI's role and impact across different aspects of life. As we better understand AI, we develop the ability to choose technologies that align with our values and goals, promoting a sense of agency and competence in a tech-centric world (Ensrud, 2024).

Build an Adaptive Mindset

Beyond understanding technology, building an adaptive mindset is crucial for thriving amidst rapid advancements. An adaptive mindset refers to having the resilience to cope with changes and the willingness to adjust strategies based on new information. This mindset is particularly important because AI is continuously evolving, driven by improvements in algorithms and data availability. In practice, an adaptive mindset encourages individuals to view challenges posed by AI adoption as opportunities for growth rather than obstacles.

For instance, a marketing professional adapting to AI-powered analytics tools might initially feel overwhelmed by their complexity. However, by approaching the learning process with curiosity and openness, they can harness these tools to derive deeper insights into consumer behavior and enhance campaign effectiveness (McGowan & Shipley, 2020). Cultivating this resilient approach not only empowers individuals to tackle technological disruptions with confidence but also positions them to leverage AI in innovative ways.

Embrace Collaboration

Embracing collaboration across disciplines is essential to maximizing the innovative potential that AI brings. AI functions most effectively when it complements human intellect, bridging gaps between diverse fields such as engineering, psychology, and art. Cross-disciplinary collaboration allows for the integration of unique perspectives and skill sets, leading to more holistic and effective solutions. Consider a project team developing an AI-based educational app: software engineers may focus on technical development, while educators contribute expertise on learning methodologies, and psychologists provide insights into cognitive processes. Such collaboration ensures that the final product is engaging, pedagogically sound, and user-friendly, catering to a broad audience including students and teachers. Encouraging collaboration also enhances communication within AI-enhanced contexts, breaking down silos and promoting the free flow of ideas (Leonardi & Neeley, 2022).

To truly adapt and excel in an AI-driven world, organizations and individuals alike must commit to creating environments that promote interdisciplinary collaboration. This involves recognizing the value of diverse viewpoints and facilitating open dialogue among team members from varied backgrounds. Organizations can achieve this by establishing cross-functional teams and encouraging participation in workshops and brainstorming sessions that spur creative thinking. Furthermore, cultivating emotional intelligence within these collaborative settings ensures that team members can effectively manage interpersonal dynamics and work together harmoniously, ultimately driving innovation forward.

Final Insights

AI is weaving itself into our daily lives, not just by making tasks easier but by opening up new possibilities for creativity and self-improvement. Whether it's through intuitive virtual assistants or productivity-boosting devices, AI is making technology more accessible to everyone. This democratization allows people from all walks of life to incorporate AI into their routines without needing deep technical knowledge. Now you can devote more time to creative pursuits because a smart device is taking care of household chores or managing your finances efficiently. It's like adding an extra pair of hands to our daily tasks, offering us more time to explore and innovate.

Moreover, AI is also changing how we work and grow. In the workplace, AI enhances human capabilities by processing data at lightning speed, providing insights that may have been missed otherwise. This means that professionals can make more informed decisions and focus on strategic thinking. For those interested in personal growth, AI-driven learning platforms offer tailored educational experiences, making learning both accessible and personalized. AI is here to enhance our lifestyles, foster creativity, and empower us as we navigate this tech-savvy world.

Conclusion

Finding balance and harmony in our busy lives can be challenging, especially when technology seems to evolve faster than we can keep up with. For many of us, AI is both a source of fascination and intimidation. The promise of AI isn't just about futuristic dreams; it's about practical, everyday solutions that significantly impact our daily lives as AI offers opportunities to transform your routines, enhance productivity, and fuel personal development.

Think about your mornings. AI allows you to start the day with less stress and more efficiency. With AI-powered devices seamlessly managing your household chores, you have more time to focus on what truly matters. As you ease into the day, these smart technologies tirelessly optimize temperature, lighting, and even reminders—all tailored to suit your lifestyle. It's not just convenience but an invitation to reclaim precious moments that might otherwise slip away unnoticed.

For busy professionals juggling endless tasks, AI offers a remarkable ally in the race against time. AI acts like a virtual assistant by anticipating your needs and suggesting improvements to your schedule. This assistant learns, adapts, and grows alongside you, offering insights and strategies that streamline your workflow. Suddenly, hours previously lost to mundane tasks are unlocked, giving you space to innovate, create, and engage more deeply with your passions.

Yet, in our enthusiasm to harness AI's potential, we must remain aware of ethical considerations. Responsible use of AI requires fairness and equality. We hold the power to influence how AI shapes society, reinforcing values that prioritize humanity. Organizations that lead by example set a precedent for others, showing us that technology, when developed and implemented ethically, can lead to thriving communities.

Embracing AI means unlocking new dimensions of self-improvement. Now you can access AI-driven financial tools that offer personalized budgeting advice, transforming how you manage your resources. Or consider leveraging health apps that monitor well-being, nudging you towards healthier habits. These applications empower you to make informed decisions, paving the way for growth and fulfillment.

Staying informed about AI advancements is crucial to navigating the evolving landscape. This proactive approach equips us with the adaptability to face technological changes confidently. The more we understand AI's capabilities, the better we can integrate them into our personal and professional lives. When we're aware of emerging trends, we gain a competitive edge and the confidence to embrace innovation.

However, to fully embrace AI we need to cultivate a mindset that thrives on learning and adaptation. By continuously expanding our knowledge of AI, we become proactive participants in shaping its future. This engagement encourages a culture of curiosity, sparking conversations that explore AI's role in diverse fields.

Embarking on this path also means acknowledging the importance of connection—bridging gaps between technology and human experience. AI isn't a solitary endeavor; it's a collaborative force that unites people from different walks of life. It encourages dialogue, promotes understanding, and nurtures empathy. Together, we can ensure AI enhances lives without compromising individuality.

Incorporating AI into our lives is about empowerment. It's about recognizing that these tools are extensions of our capabilities—a chance to amplify our strengths while addressing our challenges. As we experiment and innovate, we unlock the potential we never imagined possible.

Let's remember that AI isn't perfect. It's a tool crafted by humans, and its success depends on how responsibly we guide its development. Engaging with AI thoughtfully and deliberately allows us to shape its trajectory positively, ensuring it remains a force for good.

So, whether you're approaching AI with curiosity, seeking productivity gains, or embarking on a journey of self-discovery, know that you're not alone. You're part of a dynamic community reshaping how we live, work, and grow. Embrace AI as an ally, a partner, and a co-pilot on this exciting adventure.

Begin by incorporating small changes—adopt that smart home device, try out a productivity app, or explore AI-driven learning platforms. With each step, you'll notice how AI subtly integrates into your life, enhancing experiences and inviting you to look at the world differently.

Finally, stay inspired. Let AI's possibilities invigorate your imagination and drive your ambitions. What once seemed complex becomes accessible, and what once felt overwhelming transforms into empowerment. You have the tools, the knowledge, and the capacity to weave AI into your narrative, creating a story uniquely yours.

Embrace this era of transformation wholeheartedly because AI is here to stay—and it's here to help. Let it be a beacon guiding you toward new horizons, where potential knows no bounds, and opportunities abound. In this vast, interconnected world, the future of AI lies not only in technology but in the hands of those who dare to dream, challenge norms, and redefine what's possible.

Are you ready to be one of them?

References

Ahmad, Z. (2024, December 6). *Discover AI's role in advancing real-time language learning tools.* Tabsgi. https://www.tabsgi.com/discover-ais-role-in-advancing-real-time-language-learning-tools/

AI for tutoring: Real-time support and feedback. (2024, August 4). Redress Compliance. https://redresscompliance.com/ai-tutoring/

AI in data analytics: Transforming decision-making. (2024, April 1). Imenso Software. https://www.imensosoftware.com/blog/ai-in-data-analytics-transforming-decision-making/

AI in hiring: 7 myths you need to stop believing. (n.d.). Curately AI https://www.curately.ai/post/ai-in-hiring-7-myths-you-need-to-stop-believing

AI in project management: Streamlining tasks and automation. (2024, December). Newo.ai. https://newo.ai/insights/ai-in-project-management-streamlining-tasks-and-automation/

The AI revolution in wellness: How personalized health plans are getting smarter. (2025). The FIT Partnership. https://www.thefitpartnership.co.uk/the-ai-revolution-in-wellness/

Anglen, J. (n.d.). *AI for wealth management: Robo-advisors, investment strategies, and future trends.* Rapid Innovation. https://www.rapidinnovation.io/post/robo-advisors-transforming-investment-advice-with-ai

Artificial intelligence and productivity: Transforming the modern workplace. (2025, January 13). ESCP Business School. https://escp.eu/news/artificial-intelligence-and-productivity-transforming-modern-workplace

Baig, A., and Khan, M. (2024, March 11). *What is AI safety?* Securiti. https://securiti.ai/ai-safety/

Bieser, J. (2023, February 20). *How can AI support human creativity? Here's what a new study found.* World Economic Forum. https://www.weforum.org/stories/2023/02/ai-can-catalyze-and-inhibit-your-creativity-here-is-how/

Chiu, T.K.F., Xia, Q., Zhou, X., Chai, C.S., and Cheng, M. (2023). Systematic literature review on opportunities, challenges, and future research recommendations of artificial intelligence in education. *Computers and Education: Artificial Intelligence 4.* https://doi.org/10.1016/j.caeai.2022.100118

Clarkson, S. (2024, October 25). *Essential tools for managing tasks with your virtual assistant.* Freedom Makers. https://www.freedom-makers.com/essential-tools-for-managing-tasks-with-your-virtual-assistant

Coursera Staff. (2025, January 6). *5 AI trends to watch in 2025.* Coursera. https://www.coursera.org/articles/ai-trends

Das, M. (2024, November 19). *How AI in project management is reshaping project management?* Celoxis. https://www.celoxis.com/article/ai-in-project-management-resource-planning-execution

Dweck, C. (2016, January 13). *What having a "growth mindset" actually means.* Harvard Business Review. https://hbr.org/2016/01/what-having-a-growth-mindset-actually-means

Echeverry, C. (2024, July 12). *Personalized learning with AI: Innovations in education.* Intersog. https://intersog.com/blog/strategy/personalized-learning-with-ai/

Ensrud, K. (2024, January 17). *Navigating the new normal: Adapting in the age of AI and hybrid work models.* Chief Learning Officer. https://www.chieflearningofficer.com/2024/01/17/navigating-the-new-normal-adapting-in-the-age-of-ai-and-hybrid-work-models/

The ethical considerations of artificial intelligence (2023, May 30). Capitol Technology University. https://www.captechu.edu/blog/ethical-considerations-of-artificial-intelligence

The evolution and future of artificial intelligence: A student's guide. (n.d.). California Miramar University. https://www.calmu.edu/news/future-of-artificial-intelligence

Fabbrizio, A., Fucarino, A., Cantoia, M., De Giorgio, A., Garrido, N.D., Iuliano, E., Reis, V.M., Sausa, M., Vilaça-Alves, J., Zimatore, G., Baldari, C., and Macaluso, F. (2023). Smart devices for health and wellness applied to tele-exercise: An overview of new trends and technologies such as IoT and AI. *Healthcare 11* (12). https://doi.org/10.3390/healthcare11121805

Filipsson, F. (2024, August 6). *AI in investment management.* Redress Compliance. https://redresscompliance.com/ai-investment-management/

Generative AI in content creation: Revolutionizing workflows and boosting efficiency. (2024, December 28). Ingosa. https://www.ingosa.ai/post/generative-ai-in-content-creation-revolutionizing-workflows-and-boosting-efficiency

Girimonte, M. (2024, September 30). *The impact of AI voice on language learning.* Voices. https://www.voices.com/blog/ai-voice-language-learning/

Giordano, M. (2024, April 11). *The best personal safety devices, apps, and wearables.* Wired. https://www.wired.com/story/best-personal-safety-tech/

Haque, R., and Rubya, S. (2023). An overview of chatbot-based mobile mental health applications: Insights from app description and user reviews. *JMIR MHealth and UHealth 11.* https://doi.org/10.2196/44838

Herbert, K. (2022, January 7). *Pittsburgh is reimagining mobility.* Better Bike Shared Partnership. https://betterbikeshare.org/2022/01/07/pittsburgh-is-reimagining-mobility/

Home Energy Management System (HEMS). (2024, October 16). gridX. https://www.gridx.ai/knowledge/home-energy-management-system-hems

How artificial intelligence Is enhancing financial data security. (2024, September 24). Storific. https://www.storific.com/blog/how-artificial-intelligence-is-enhancing-financial-data-security

The impact of artificial intelligence on virtual tutoring. (n.d.). Vnaya. https://www.vnaya.com/blog/The-Impact-of-Artificial-Intelligence-on-Virtual-Tutoring

Integrating AI into your creative workflow; Best practices for boosting productivity and innovation. (n.d.). Pro Edu. https://proedu.com/blogs/photoshop-skills/integrating-ai-into-your-creative-workflow-best-practices-for-boosting-productivity-and-innovation?srsltid=AfmBOop9IwFISD8HgTt61KF2oXsZ1jPP3GcUm7xCPX3eqlhaLSpo08Cg

Iyer, L.S. (2021). AI enabled applications towards intelligent transportation. *Transportation Engineering 5.* https://doi.org/10.1016/j.treng.2021.100083

Jantz-Sell, T. (2024, February 25). *Save energy with smart home products.* Energy Star. https://www.energystar.gov/products/ask-the-experts/save-energy-smart-home-products

Kumar, A. (2025, January 10). *These robotic home helpers can vacuum, mop, wash windows, mow your lawn, and even clean itself.* CNET. https://www.cnet.com/home/kitchen-and-household/these-robotic-home-helpers-can-vacuum-mop-wash-windows-mow-your-lawn-and-even-clean-itself/

Le, N.H. (2024, November 14). *Guide to gamification in EdTech: Key elements, successful strategies, & top examples.* SmartDev. https://smartdev.com/guide-to-gamification-in-edtech-key-elements-successful-strategies-top-examples/

Leonardi, P., and Neely, T. (2022). *The digital mindset: What it really takes to thrive in the age of data, algorithms, and AI.* Harvard Business Review Press.

Lim, P. (2025, January 9). *Debunked: 4 myths about AI-assisted decision-making in the boardroom.* Diligent. https://jp.diligent.com/resources/blog/4-myths-about-ai-in-the-boardroom

Lumenalta. (2024, October 13). *Ethical considerations of AI.* Lumenalta. https://lumenalta.com/insights/ethical-considerations-of-ai

Manoharan, A. (2024, June 4). *Next-gen education: 8 strategies leveraging AI in learning platforms.* Forbes. https://www.forbes.com/councils/forbestechcouncil/2024/06/04/next-gen-education-8-strategies-leveraging-ai-in-learning-platforms/

McGowan, H.E., and Shipley, C. (2020). *The adaptation advantage: Let go, learn fast, and thrive in the future of work.* Wiley.

Malec, M. (2024, December 2). *Generative AI statistics: Insights and emerging trends for 2025.* HatchWorksAI. https://hatchworks.com/blog/gen-ai/generative-ai-statistics/

Nine ethical AI principles for organizations to follow. (2023, January 10). Cogent Infotech. https://www.cogentinfo.com/resources/9-ethical-ai-principles-for-organizations-to-follow

Olawade, D.B., Wada, O.Z., Odetayo, A., David-Olawade, A.C., Asaolu, F., and Eberhardt, J. (2024). Enhancing mental health with artificial intelligence: Current trends and future prospects. *Journal of Medicine, Surgery, and Public Health 3.* https://doi.org/10.1016/j.glmedi.2024.100099

Ovick, B., and Wu, C.H. (2024, October 25). *CFPB finalized rule 1033 to protect data privacy: What to know.* Skyflow. https://www.skyflow.com/post/cfpb-finalized-rule-1033-to-protect-data-privacy-what-to-know

Petrenko, V. (2025, January 6). *AI and transportation: How AI Technology Streamlines Traffic.* Litslink. https://litslink.com/blog/ai-and-transportation

Poth, R.D. (2023, October 20). *7 AI tools that help teachers work more efficiently.* Edutopia. https://www.edutopia.org/article/7-ai-tools-that-help-teachers-work-more-efficiently/

Sahota, N. (2024, July 20). *AI shields kids by revolutionizing child safety and online protection.* Forbes. https://www.forbes.com/sites/neilsahota/2024/07/20/ai-shields-kids-by-revolutionizing-child-safety-and-online-protection/

Schneider Electric launches AI-powered home energy management feature for Wiser Home. (2024). Schneider Electric. https://www.se.com/ww/en/about-us/newsroom/news/press-releases/schneider-electric-launches-ai-powered-home-energy-management-feature-for-wiser-home-66d6bac4d6b0eff3580dc113

Senyk, A. (2024, December 23). *Full guide of AI voice assistant for your business: Key types, applications, and reasons to invest.* SPSoft. https://spsoft.com/tech-insights/everything-about-ai-voice-assistant/

Singh, J. (2024, November 13). *How AI is shaping the future of remote work and virtual collaboration.* FPGA Insights. https://fpgainsights.com/artificial-intelligence/how-ai-is-shaping-the-future-of-remote-work/

Smart travel planner: How AI is revolutionizing travel planning. (2024, January 9). iPlan.ai. https://iplan.ai/smart-travel-planner-2-p1610/

Terekhov, V. (2024, May 8). *How to integrate AI in public transport systems for efficiency.* Attract Group. https://attractgroup.com/blog/ai-in-public-transport/

Top 10 benefits of a virtual assistant. (n.d.). Intellect Outsource. https://www.intellectoutsource.com/blog/benefits-of-virtual-assistants

Tsymbal, T. (2024, December 26). *Voice assistants: The profit, accessibility, and speed trifecta for modern businesses.* Master of Code. https://masterofcode.com/blog/voice-assistants-use-cases-examples-for-business

The use of AI in real-time data analysis and decision-making. (2023, April 27). University of the Cumberlands. https://www.ucumberlands.edu/blog/use-ai-real-time-data-analysis-and-decision-making

Venkatesh, B. (2024, May 15). *Transforming trip planning with AI-powered travel advisors.* Flyfish. https://www.flyfish.ai/blog/ai-powered-travel-advisors/

Verma, D. (2023, February 28). *AI inventions – the ethical and societal implications.* ManagingIP. https://www.managingip.com/article/2bc988k82fc0ho408vwu8/expert-analysis/ai-inventions-the-ethical-and-societal-implications

Verma, A. (2024, October 19). *Smart roads: How GenAI and AIML are revolutionizing traffic control.* Medium. https://medium.com/@ajayverma23/smart-roads-how-genai-and-aiml-are-revolutionizing-traffic-control-fbdfa033f644

Vujadinovic, V.L., Damnjanovic, A., Cakic, A., Petkovic, D.R., Prelevic, M., Pantovic, V., Stojanovic, M., Vidojevic, D., Vranjes, D., and Bodolo, I. (2024). AI-driven approach for enhancing sustainability in urban public transportation. *Sustainability 16* (17). https://doi.org/10.3390/su16177763

Walter, Y. (2024). Embracing the future of artificial intelligence in the classroom: The relevance of AI literacy, prompt engineering, and critical thinking in modern education. *International Journal of Educational Technology in Higher Education 21* (15). https://doi.org/10.1186/s41239-024-00448-3

What are the AI Tools for career development programs in 2025? (2024, December 16). Disco. https://www.disco.co/blog/ai-tools-for-career-development-programs

What is a smart home and what are the benefits? (2025). Constellation. https://www.constellation.com/energy-101/what-is-a-smart-home.html

What is the history of artificial intelligence (AI)? (n.d.). Tableau. https://www.tableau.com/data-insights/ai/history

Wilhelm, J. (2024, July 8). *Responsible AI – Privacy & Security.* Infused Innovations. https://infusedinnovations.com/blog/responsible-ai-privacy-security

Zawacki-Richter, O., Marin, V.I., Bond, M., and Gouverneur, F. (2019). Systematic review of research on artificial intelligence application in higher education - where are the educators? *International Journal of Educational Technology in Higher Education 16* (39). https://doi.org/10.1186/s41239-019-0171-0